ESL CENTER

Cambridge English Readers

Level 6

Series editor: Philip Prowse

The Way Home

Sue Leather

CAMBRIDGE
UNIVERSITY PRESS

CAMBRIDGE
UNIVERSITY PRESS

University Printing House, Cambridge CB2 8BS, United Kingdom

Cambridge University Press is part of the University of Cambridge.

It furthers the University's mission by disseminating knowledge in the pursuit of education, learning and research at the highest international levels of excellence.

www.cambridge.org
Information on this title: www.cambridge.org/9780521543620

First published 2004
Reprinted 2016

Printed in the United Kingdom by Hobbs the Printers Ltd

A catalogue record for this publication is available from the British Library

Cover by Adventure House

And when you had thought to travel outwards
you will come to the centre of your existence
Joseph Campbell

To the memory of my dad, Des, who gave me this love of
travelling outwards, and so much more.

ISBN 978-0-521-54362-0 Paperback

Contents

The Way Home

You can go home again . . . so long as you understand that home is a place where you have never been.

Ursula le Guin, *The Dispossessed*

'Damn it!' said Jake, coming out of his study into the bedroom, where Alex was packing her bags.

'What's the matter?' she asked, looking up through her dark brown shoulder-length hair.

'It's this stupid film,' said Jake, sitting down heavily on the bed in front of her and sighing.

Jake had been working on a story for a new film and his deadline was just a few days away. His handsome face was lined and he looked fed up. He was finding the writing hard and he was tired. Alex tried to care. But behind her husband through the window she could see New York shining in the late-afternoon autumn sunlight. She was busy preparing for her trip to England; her flight was leaving later that evening. She felt a longing to be gone, to be somewhere else.

'I'll never get it right!' Jake went on.

'Of course you will,' said Alex weakly. 'You know you always do.' They both noticed the slight annoyance in her voice.

There was a silence.

'So, er, when you come back, maybe we can take a vacation?' Jake's voice sounded hopeful. 'I mean,' he went on, 'just a couple of days, a long weekend perhaps. Maybe we can go to Palm Springs?'

Alex's eyes wandered to the tall silver buildings set against the pale blue sky.

'Maybe,' she said, smiling and trying to make it sound like it was a real possibility, but not managing it. Jake got up quickly and went back to his study, shaking his head.

Alex tried to wipe the confused look on Jake's face from her mind and carried on packing. As usual, she was finding it difficult to decide which clothes to take. Though she was a buyer for an international fashion house and travelled a lot, she never found it easy to pack. And now it was even more difficult. She was going to the north of England to visit her parents; she was going home, for the first time in over ten years. She was going home to deal with the past. She was thirty-two years old.

A mix of autumn and winter clothes, she decided in the end. You never knew what the weather would be like in England. And she loved knitwear, especially woollen sweaters. Not everyone could wear knitwear, but she could.

She finished her packing, then felt tired and lay down on the bed. Her eyes looked up at the landscape painting on the wall opposite the bed. It was of the moors around the place where she had grown up, a copy of a famous painting. She loved it. She'd found it by accident in a second-hand shop on a work visit to London a couple of years ago. From time to time she would look at it and realise how much she missed those hills, that landscape. Her memories of it were like precious jewels that she kept locked inside a box; sometimes she opened the lid and they surprised her with their beauty. 'My place,' she said, out loud.

The moors in the north of England were wild and as a child she had loved them. The moor near her home was called Randle Moor and she had spent a lot of time there walking and discovering its secrets. Now, in her dreams she walked the moors of her childhood. They fed her imagination and her desires.

In England, she loved packing a sandwich and a drink and walking out into the countryside for an hour or two. You could do that at home; the countryside was just *there*. She loved America, but it was so hard to go out for a walk here, she thought. The distances were so huge. When her American friends asked her what the moors were like, she was often lost for words. 'They're just beautiful, wild in their own special way.' She often added, 'Think of Emily Brontë – you know *Wuthering Heights*.' Most people had at least seen the old film.

She suddenly jumped up from the bed, took her old leather walking boots out of the wardrobe, and put them in her suitcase. Perhaps she would want to go for a walk over her lovely moors.

She lay down again and closed her eyes. She still had time for a rest before she had to go to JFK airport to catch her flight to London. But though she felt tired, she couldn't sleep. Her mind turned to thoughts of Jake. She felt guilty about not wanting to talk to him. They had met eight years before at a party in Denver. He had shone like a light in the room. He was very handsome and very charming. He had black hair and the most beautiful brown eyes. He had walked up to Alex and offered her a drink.

'Before I met you,' he said, giving her a martini, 'I felt like a man with a fork in a world of soup.'

'That's definitely a line from a film,' she said and laughed.

They had talked all evening and most of the night. She felt comfortable with him. Comfortable, but excited. And he *was* very good-looking, a bit like Andy Garcia.

They had started seeing a lot of each other immediately and she soon realised that their interest in films wasn't the only thing they had in common. She fell in love quickly and totally and they got married within six months. Then they moved to New York; it was better for both their careers and they liked the energy of the place.

When they got married, she felt complete. Jake was everything she'd always wanted and, incredibly, he wasn't scared of her success, because he was successful too. Now she had her career, an apartment in Manhattan, great friends and Jake. Before she met him she had felt that she would always be searching, travelling, that somehow she would never find her own home, that she would never find her place. But now she felt settled.

Settled, she thought to herself. So where had it gone wrong?

*   *   *

A few hours later Alex was sitting in a quiet corner of the departure lounge at JFK airport waiting for her flight to London Heathrow. She felt a little better now that she was on her way, now that she was on her own. It was always easier when she was travelling, when she was going somewhere else.

The flight had been delayed for over an hour. She took out a thriller and tried to read, but she couldn't concentrate. So she just sat and watched the people walking by and sitting in the departure lounge. She always liked to look at the way people dressed; she often found herself criticising their style, their clothes. It was because of her job, she guessed. She just couldn't stand badly-dressed people. Didn't they know that the way you looked said so much about you?

One of the things that had attracted her to Jake in the first place was that he dressed well, Alex thought. She started reading again but found herself still unable to concentrate. Yes, Jake dressed well, but not as well as Stefano. Ah yes, Stefano. It had started two years ago when she met Stefano.

Two years ago . . . She remembered that she had been sitting in the departure lounge at Milan Malpensa airport. She'd been to a big fashion show and was flying to Paris to do some buying before going home to New York. They called her flight and, as usual, she waited until everyone else had boarded; she just carried on sitting there. She hated queuing up; what was the point? You had your seat already. You might as well wait until everyone else had got on.

'*Mi pare che viagga molto.*' said a man's voice behind her. She turned round and looked right into the eyes of the most beautiful man.

'Er, I'm sorry,' she said, 'my Italian isn't very good.' She looked at him. He had to be Italian. He was dressed in that way only Italian men know how, in an Armani suit and a pale peach-coloured shirt that set off his dark skin perfectly.

'Oh, I'm sorry,' he said in perfect English. 'I was just

saying that you are an experienced traveller. Me too, I always wait until the end of the queue.' He smiled and held out his hand. 'Stefano, Stefano Cabianca. And you are?'

'Alex Kramer,' she said, shaking his hand.

They started chatting. He was also in the fashion business and also flying to Paris to do some buying. When they finally got on the plane, he changed his seat to sit next to her. They talked about everything, but mostly fashion and their favourite designers. Of course he loved the Italian designers and she was a great fan of the British ones.

'But the British designers,' he said, jokingly, 'they are so strange . . . so weird . . . I mean, look at Vivienne Westwood!'

She laughed. 'Yes,' she said, 'but look at Stella McCartney and John Galliano. Nobody could deny they're great designers!'

They had a lively conversation about Alexander McQueen. They agreed that Gucci had become too commercial. And, yes, Versace was not what it had been before Gianni Versace's death. They drank a glass of wine together. It all seemed harmless, but she was aware that she was very attracted to him.

Then, about fifteen minutes before they landed at Charles de Gaulle airport, he said to her, 'I am staying at a hotel in Paris tonight, near Notre Dame. You don't have to fly to New York until tomorrow. We are getting on so well. It would be such a pity to say goodbye now. Why don't you stay with me?'

She looked at him. He was asking her to stay with him at a hotel. He was asking her to be unfaithful to her husband. It wasn't totally unexpected, but she felt her face getting hot. 'I . . . I'm not sure.' There was a moment of hesitation, but it was only a moment. It was true that her flight to New York wasn't until the next evening. She had to be in Paris that night. 'OK,' she said, smiling, 'why not?' And then came into her mind the terrible thought, 'No one will ever know.'

Since that night she had seen Stefano six times; they would meet up when they were travelling and their schedules coincided. In Paris, Rome, Milan. She still loved her husband, but she couldn't tell him about her affair. She also didn't know how to stop her betrayal.

Now, sitting in the departure lounge at JFK, she had a feeling that was both comforting and disturbing. She was beginning to believe that only her journey home would help her to bring her betrayal to an end.

*   *   *

At last Alex was able to board the plane for the flight to London Heathrow. She sat down in her business class window seat and within moments they were in the air, the features of the earth disappearing fast. Alex ordered a gin and tonic from the air steward and tried to relax.

She was going home, she thought, back to the past. The plane was a Boeing 747, like the one that had brought her father back from Africa so many years ago. He had to work there for twelve months. Alex was ten years old.

'What's it like in Africa, Daddy?' she asked him on the way home. Alex had gone with her mother to Manchester airport in a taxi to pick him up. It was a great treat. They wore their best clothes. Her mother wore a smart blue suit; Alex was wearing her favourite shiny black shoes.

'Well, it's difficult to say . . . but very hot,' her father said, smiling.

She sat next to him in the taxi; he smelled of after-shave and far-off lands.

She smiled now, thinking about her father; she was very like him and she became more like him as she got older. They both loved travelling so much. For most of her childhood her father had been abroad and she had missed him. Sometimes she would sit in her little bedroom and stare at the world globe he had given her one Christmas. She would spin it around, find the country where he was, and try to imagine what it was like. Then she would shut her eyes tight and try to picture his face, his blond curls and his smile. Sometimes it was hard to remember what he looked like, so she would take out the family photographs and stare at him, trying to make herself remember his face for ever.

She loved having a father who worked abroad, though. The girls at school had fathers who had jobs in the factories and offices in the little industrial town where they lived. Their fathers were everyday fathers, while hers was a magical one. She was different, special because of him. She had never lost that feeling that he made her special.

Yes, she had really loved it. Until that hot summer's day two years later when she was twelve years old.

*   *   *

At Heathrow Airport Alex went to the car hire desk and picked up the keys to a silver-coloured Ford. She was always a bit nervous of driving on the left. When she came to England for work, it was usually just to London so she used taxis or the Underground; she never drove. However, she managed to find the M25, the motorway which goes around the edge of London, and followed it until she turned onto the road heading north.

Once she was on the motorway, she began to relax. The road ahead was blue-grey, the colour of the North Sea on a cold day. It was late afternoon, and the autumn light was soft. The fields on either side of the road stretched as far as you could see, dull and wet. She hadn't got to the hills yet; the world was still flat. She was lost in thought, thinking back twenty years, back to when she was twelve years old.

She was running home from school. They'd been given the afternoon off for some reason. It was a warm June day, almost hot, and the sky was powder blue with little lines of white silk across it. She was thinking that she'd go home and change out of her tight, heavy school uniform and then take her fishing net down to the lake. She was free!

She was running, all excited, through the fields. If she went that way, she could see her house from a long way off. As she got nearer, Alex saw her mother through an upstairs window, her bedroom window. Alex looked hard. She could also see the shape of someone else through the window.

It was a man's shape, tall and broad, not her father because he was abroad, working. She went a little closer to the house and saw a red car parked outside. Then, in a flash, she understood. She saw it all. She was only twelve but she understood. She stopped dead. The world became still. The house, the car, the little garden path that led from the gate up to the front door, everything seemed to hang motionless in the lazy summer air. Tears started to hurt her eyes and she turned around and ran, ran off into the moors. Sometimes it seems like she has never stopped running.

That's when she really got to love the moors, after seeing her mother with that man. Before that, they'd just been there, like the factory chimneys. But then they became her friends, a place where she could go to escape. Randle Moor especially became her place. A kind of escape from the storm. An escape from her secret.

She still didn't know how she managed not to say anything to anyone, especially to her mother. A twelve-year-old child finds it hard to keep something like that inside. But she did, and a terrible hatred grew inside her against her mother, and a dreadful fear that her mother would leave her father. 'Then,' Alex thought, 'I'll have to go and live with Mum and that man.' But nothing happened, and she just kept everything she knew inside, hard and unforgiving. And she hated her mother for betraying her father, hated her for making her feel like that. She hated her so much that she had never told anyone about it, not even Jake.

Alex left home to go to college as soon as she could, when she was eighteen, and she'd never gone back. After college she'd gone to the United States for a visit and she'd stayed there. Since then she'd seen her mother and father just a few times – in the States, in London and when she got married to Jake in Denver. But she'd always managed to avoid going home.

But now, since Stefano, she understood. She understood that betrayal could happen, that disloyalty was not that difficult. Finally, she understood her mother. It was time to go home.

*　　*　　*

'. . . and then I just ran off to the moors.' Alex was calm when she actually talked to her mother about it. She supposed it was because she'd gone over the scene so many times in her mind.

They were sitting at her mother's kitchen table, where everything important had always been discussed. Alex's father had gone out for a walk with the dog. Alex had told her mother what she'd seen that day twenty years ago.

'I often wondered if you knew,' said her mother, her hands held tightly together in front of her. 'You became so . . . distant.'

Though Alex was calm, her mother was upset. As usual, her first reaction had been to put the kettle on and make tea. So they sat there at the table drinking milky tea and talking about unfaithfulness.

'I suppose I was lonely, your father was away so much,' her mother went on. 'Oh, I know it was wrong, but these things happen, you know . . .'

'I know,' Alex said, managing a smile. She took a deep breath and told her mother about Jake and Stefano. She was surprised to find that it came out so quickly and easily.

'Well,' Alex's mother said, 'you know what's best. Jake is such a lovely man.' Alex remembered that at the wedding, her mother had got on extremely well with Jake.

'And so is Dad,' Alex said.

'Yes,' said her mother, smiling. 'You know, I think one

thing you realise as you get older is that it's really hard to find something that good, and really easy to lose it.'

'But you didn't lose Dad . . .'

'No,' said her mother firmly, 'and you won't lose Jake, not if you really want to keep him.'

Alex looked at her mother. 'Does Dad know?' she asked. 'I mean did you . . .'

Her mother nodded. 'Yes,' she said. 'I told him. I wanted to be honest. And I wanted to know that the love we had for each other was enough to get us through.'

*   *   *

Alex stayed for a week. She and her mother talked a lot, laughed a lot and cried a little. Alex was happy, though she knew that at the end of the week, she would have a difficult decision to make. Soon she would see Jake and she had to think about him, about the future.

The day before she had to go back to New York, Alex decided to take a walk over Randle Moor, the place she'd loved so much as a child. She had to decide. Would she tell Jake about what she had done, and risk losing him?

She drove to the lake that lay at the foot of the moor. Leaving the little car in the car park, she put on her walking boots and set off up the steep path that led from the shore to the top of the moor. It was such a luxury, she thought, just being able to walk in the countryside. But it was hard going; the small stones that covered the path were loose and slippery. In places on the path there was thick mud from the rain a few nights ago and she had to go back and find another way up to the top. There were only a few other walkers out that early November day and they were far away from her on the other side of the moor. The air was cold and there were patches of snow on the hills. As she made her way slowly up the hillside, the world became a gentler, quieter place, until the only sound she could hear was of her own heavy breathing.

She walked on, enveloped by moor now, the lake and the rest of the valley hidden from view. The moor held her safe in its arms and she felt again her old love of this beautiful landscape. 'My place,' she thought. The hills could be bare and wild, but they offered a kind of comfort to her because she knew them so well. She had been away for so long, but still they were part of her. She knew their secret places.

Finally the moor began to open out, unfolding its arms and setting her free. Now she had a view of part of the lake, grey-green and silent in the valley, clear like a mirror. She stopped and looked down, enjoying the silence that lay across the valley and the sound of blood beating in her ears.

She took a water bottle out of her pack, knelt down on the ground and took a long drink. The cool water tasted of earth. Suddenly she had a flash of memory, like a faded photograph. She was a child again, of no more than ten or eleven, before she lost her innocence. It was a long hot summer's day and she was walking over the moors. She had brought a bottle of water from home and took a drink from time to time. She remembered the feeling of being completely alone up here. It was a delicious feeling and one that she still enjoyed so much. It was part of her.

Alex shook her head, chasing the memory away. After a few moments rest, she started off again up the moors. The landscape began to open out like a magic carpet, slowly revealing the little houses and farms on the other side of the lake. The sheep and cows on the farms looked like those toy animals that children play with, she thought. Then, slowly, the village in the valley came into view, a soft brown collection of stone buildings. Then came the factory chimneys of the big town in the distance, the chimneys that had been the background to her childhood. Next the lake revealed its true extent, uncurling itself like a giant snake. Finally the full beauty of the landscape lay there beneath her. She stood at the top of the moor, feeling the silence and the moment. The view was like a picture from a child's storybook, unreal and shining. Early-winter sunlight fell on the far shore of the lake, making the green of the hills glow. The air sang, pure and clear. She thought of her mother and father down below in their tiny house in the tiny town.

She smiled. Distance makes everything clearer; you can only see the whole when you're far enough away. Life is like this, she thought, this moving away, this distancing. There was a time when these people, this town, this landscape were your whole world, your universe, everything you knew. And this world had pressed around you and made its mark, deep and permanent, a mark that went with you everywhere. And, in some way in some small place inside, in the deepest part of yourself, this first world would always be your destination. A world that you would always long for, but that would always be hard to find again.

She thought about Jake. Yes, distance made everything clear. She knew now that she could go back to New York and talk to him. That she *had* to talk to him. She knew

17

that she could tell him what had happened, what she had done . . . and ask his forgiveness. Ask him in the same way that her mother had asked her father for forgiveness. Tell him that she still loved him, that she would always love him. She knew that she could finally stop running away.

Yes, she thought, smiling, she really was going home. And as she stood there an awareness came to her that as she had travelled ever further outwards, she had always been looking for the way back to this, her first world. Her place. And that now at last she had found the path that led to the house far below in the valley. She had finally found the way home.

The Nature of Truth

It was 8.30 on an early May morning, and Annie Sanderson was at Rome's Termini station, ticket in hand, waiting for her train to Bologna.

Even so early in the morning, it was already hot; Annie could feel the sweat running down the back of her neck. It was going to be another day like yesterday, she thought, when she had given a talk at a literature conference. The room, in the Palazzo Livio, had been uncomfortably sticky. Her audience, mostly writers and professors from the English literature department of the university, had sweated through the hour and a half. Her talk, on her new novel *The Nature of Truth*, had been well received, though she wondered how they had been able to concentrate for so long in that heat. She herself had drunk two whole jugs of water.

In spite of the heat, it was wonderful to be back in Italy. Annie looked down at the grass and the little pink and yellow flowers beside the railway line and smiled. It looked like some sleepy rural village station instead of the capital city's main railway station. She loved this country; it was full of these charming contrasts.

The Bologna train pulled into platform seven. She took her seat in first class, reserved for her by her publisher. Yes, things had certainly changed since she had first come to Italy as a poor student twenty years ago. Then she had sat in third class; now she was travelling in style. Last night she had slept in a five-star hotel and had dinner at *Il Coliseo*, one of Rome's top restaurants, with some of Italy's most famous writers. She'd come a long way and she couldn't help but feel pleased with herself.

Annie sat back in her window seat to enjoy the train journey, taking out her notebook and pen as she always did on these occasions. She placed them carefully on the little table in front of her. You never knew when you might have an idea, a thought. Her huge success as a novelist came partly from this discipline. When she had first started writing fifteen years ago, she had always assumed that she would remember the ideas that came to her in the middle of the night or on a journey. But experience had taught her that she didn't. She would wake up in the morning unable to remember anything. It was very annoying to know that you had had a wonderful idea, but couldn't for the life of you remember what it was.

And now she certainly *was* successful, thought Annie, as she opened *La Repubblica*, the daily newspaper given to all first-class passengers. She quickly found a review of yesterday's event in the 'Cultura' pages. '*La romanziera inglesa, Annie Sanderson*,' she read. The English novelist! Though this was Annie's fifth book in four years, she still felt terribly excited when she saw her name in the newspapers. And she could read Italian well enough to see that the reviewer liked both her and her book. She even read the word '*bella*'. Beautiful! Well, it always helped if the reviewer thought you were attractive, especially if the reviewer was an Italian man! But even more satisfying were the comments on her work. He called her 'the most important English novelist since Iris Murdoch'. Annie smiled a broad smile. To be mentioned in the same sentence as Iris Murdoch was great praise. She read on: 'Annie Sanderson writes with great energy and honesty about one of the major problems of our time – the nature of truth. The philosophical . . .'

Annie sighed and put the newspaper down. 'Serious' reviewers in 'serious' newspapers always went on about philosophy and they always got very boring. Why couldn't they just enjoy the stories? As a writer, stories were what really interested Annie – and her readers. She looked through the window at the suburbs of Rome speeding by. There were thousands, millions of stories out there among the streets and apartment blocks. Each one of those people going to work or taking the children to school had their own story. In some ways, she thought, it was easy to write stories; they were all around you. It was the writer's job to collect them, make them interesting, bring them to life, make them *mean* something . . .

She turned back to the train compartment, which was almost full by now. Her fellow passengers mostly looked like business people, wearing dark blue suits and carrying briefcases and mobile phones. Damn the mobile phone, she thought; it should be banned. Only yesterday one had gone off in the middle of her talk. Annie had stared hard at the short fat man with the phone until he had run out of the room, red-faced and muttering, '*Me dispiace* . . . I'm sorry.' It happened so much these days.

Here on the train there were stories too, she thought. She could see a young man and an older woman travelling together a little further down. They looked like mother and son. Though Annie couldn't really hear them, she thought the woman talked to him like she was his mother. She had that motherly way of not really listening to what he was saying. Annie imagined their story – on a family visit to a dying relative perhaps. The mother was well-dressed and elegant, in a very Roman way, all big hair and gold jewellery. The boy was in his early twenties and completely beautiful. He had great dark eyes with long eyelashes, olive skin and high cheekbones. Annie found it hard not to stare.

Annie thought back to her first visit to Italy. She was a university student studying art at Cambridge and she had spent a term in Florence. It was her first real visit abroad, apart from family holidays to France, and she had found everything in Italy so beautiful. The people, the clothes, the architecture, the paintings . . . the food. And everything set off by that wonderful light, the lovely clear, sparkling light of southern Europe, so different from home. English light was so soft and grey, so *ordinary* somehow. The full light of the Mediterranean was much more passionate, and it had brought out the passionate side of Annie. She had fallen completely in love with it all. She had been an unsophisticated twenty-year-old English girl from cold, grey Liverpool. How could she not have fallen in love with Italy? And Italian men . . .

Yes, there was no doubt that Annie had a weakness, no a passion, for handsome men. She smiled to herself as her mind wandered back to an Italian boyfriend she had had in Florence. Carmine, his name was. Ah, yes, Carmine. He had curly black hair and dark brown eyes. Very good-looking, what young people in England called 'drop-dead gorgeous'. And his skin was so brown compared to hers. 'Annie,' he would say to her, in his charming Italian accent, 'you have skin white like mozzarella – you know Italian cheese.' Apart from the fact that he was handsome and the mozzarella comparison, Annie couldn't remember anything much about Carmine. He was just one in a long line of handsome men she had known.

The line about the mozzarella made her think again about her book, *The Nature of Truth*, because she had one of her main characters saying it. Yes, she thought, the nature of truth was an interesting subject. The novel was about a relationship between a man and a woman, as always. Was it possible to be faithful to one person and was it always necessary to tell the truth? Indeed, was the truth always the best thing? Wasn't it kinder sometimes not to tell the truth, or even to tell a lie? This was the philosophical question that the reviewers had talked about. And of course, although her characters had discussed it at length – 550 pages to be exact – there was no real conclusion. There was never really any conclusion in an Annie Sanderson novel, but readers seemed to love the stories and reviewers loved the 'philosophical' ideas. She herself . . .

'Annie!' It's Annie Sanderson, isn't it?' A woman's sharp voice disturbed her thoughts.

Annie jumped and looked up. Standing in front of her was a plump, middle-aged woman with short dark hair and a large smile.

'God, Annie,' the woman said loudly, 'I was wondering if it was you. I walked past twice just to make sure. But it *is* you, isn't it?' Annie stared hard at the woman, trying to work out who she was. The other passengers looked around.

'Do you remember me? It's Jane – Jane Thomson,' continued the woman. 'I was sitting right down the other end and I . . .' Her voice tailed off.

Annie blinked and thought. Then it came to her. 'Ah,' she said, suddenly. 'Of *course*. Jane, how are you?' Jane Thomson had been a friend at Cambridge; Annie hadn't seen her for almost twenty years. The plump, plain woman in front of her looked quite different from the slim, even thin girl Annie had known all those years ago. But there was something about the eyes, and the voice was unmistakable.

'Well, it's not Thomson any more. It's de Angelo, but . . .' said the woman.

Annie smiled broadly, relieved that she had remembered the woman. 'How wonderful to see you! Look, why don't you sit here,' she said, pointing to the empty seat across from her.

'Oh,' said Jane, 'it might be someone else's . . .'

'Oh, don't worry,' said Annie. 'If someone gets on you can always go back to your seat – or they can take yours.'

The woman still looked anxious. Just then a young man in a crisp uniform appeared selling drinks and snacks.

'Look, would you at least have a coffee?' said Annie.

Jane Thomson nodded. 'Well, all right. An espresso, please,' she said.

Annie ordered and paid for two espressos. As Jane sat down, Annie started to remember something else about Jane and about that man she had married immediately after university. Wasn't his name James? Ah yes, James, Annie remembered. He was a very good-looking young man.

'So,' said Annie, stirring sugar into the thick black liquid and shutting James out of her mind, 'what have you been doing for the past twenty years?'

Jane Thomson laughed. 'I could say the same to you! What are you doing in Italy? Do you live here?'

Annie shook her head and explained that she was a writer. She told Jane about the book and her tour of major Italian cities.

'So! You're famous!' said Jane.

'Well, I . . .' Annie tried to show some modesty, but she did like the word 'famous'.

'But I always knew you were creative,' Jane continued. 'How wonderful for you. I never get time to read these days but I must look out for your books.' Finally she added, 'Are you rich as well as famous?'

'Well . . .' said Annie, laughing at Jane's directness, 'not really, but I hope to be. And what about you? You must live here . . .' Jane's direct questioning was not very English, she thought; she must have been here for quite some time.

Jane confirmed Annie's guess. 'Yes,' she said. 'I came here about fifteen years ago. I came to get away from England really . . .' She paused, almost waiting for Annie to interrupt her, but Annie didn't. 'Then I got a job here in a museum. I met Pietro, and we got married, had children . . . and well, you know.'

At university Jane had studied art too and had specialised in art history. Annie remembered that as a student Jane had been crazy about Italian Renaissance art. It was no surprise that she was working in a museum. Annie wondered what had happened to James, but decided it was best to leave him out of the conversation.

'Do you live in Rome, then?' asked Annie.

'No, in Padova. Have you been there?' Jane asked.

Annie shook her head. 'No, but I've read about it in the guidebook. It must be really interesting,' she said.

'It is,' said Jane. 'You should visit some time.' Her voice was flat, lacking in feeling. It was almost like she was a city guide talking to a group of tourists. She added, 'Padova itself is a quiet, sleepy town, but nice if you want a rest.'

Jane Thomson made the place where she lived sound beautiful but very unexciting. Annie couldn't help thinking that it must be her life that was dull.

'And you're going there now?' asked Annie.

'No, not until tomorrow,' Jane said. 'I've been in Rome to talk to a museum there and now I'm going to Vernio.'

'Vernio?'

'It's a small town between Florence and Bologna,' Jane explained. 'There's a wealthy businessman there who wants to sell some valuable early-eighteenth-century art. I'll stay there tonight and then go home to Padova tomorrow.'

'So you're quite busy,' said Annie.

'Well, not really,' said Jane flatly. 'I have a trip about once a month, usually to another museum. I just work part-time, you know. The kids are still at school and I'm at home quite a lot of the time.'

Annie looked at Jane's plump face. Since she had sat down and started talking about her life, Jane Thomson had changed, Annie thought. Her shoulders had dropped and her face was no longer bright and smiling. She looked plumper somehow, more middle-aged and tired. Annie's writer's curiosity made her want to know more, made her want to know Jane's story.

'How old are the kids?' she asked.

'Twelve and eight,' Jane replied. 'Difficult ages.'

'And your husband, Pietro . . . What does he do?' asked Annie.

'Oh, he, well, what can I say?' said Jane, and again her voice was flat. 'He's an architect. He makes a lot of money. We have a comfortable life.'

Well, thought Annie, you could say he was handsome, or wonderfully kind or just nice, but instead you choose to say he's an architect and that you're 'comfortable'. Comfortable was the kind of word you might use to describe an old pair of shoes, or a favourite armchair. She looked at her old university friend for signs of enthusiasm about her marriage, but she didn't see any. Well, just another disappointed middle-aged woman, thought Annie. She looked out of the window at the landscape. The countryside had opened out to green rolling hills and trees here and there. Suddenly she lost all curiosity about the woman in front of her. Jane seemed rather boring and flat. Annie wished she was alone again to enjoy the silence and the journey.

Her wish was granted briefly. Jane got up. 'Won't be a minute,' she said, holding her handbag tightly and moving off in the direction of the toilet.

Annie enjoyed the quiet and the light on the sloping world outside the window.

A few moments later Jane was back and there was noise again.

'Do you remember James?' she said, as soon as she had sat down.

'James?' said Annie, trying to keep calm, trying to stop herself from going red.

27

'Yes, James. You remember,' said Jane, leaning forward. 'We went out together at university, oh for years. I was with him when you knew me.'

'Oh yes,' said Annie. 'James. Yes . . .'

'Well, you'll never guess what happened with him,' said Jane.

'Er . . . no,' said Annie.

'Well,' she started, 'we got married almost immediately after university and we bought a house in Notting Hill. You remember that he was a journalist?'

Annie nodded. She also remembered that James had studied law at Cambridge, mainly because his father was a judge and had wanted his son to follow in his footsteps. But James couldn't stand law, and when he left university he got a job with a major newspaper. He'd always had a passion for writing.

'Yes, well,' said Jane, 'his thing was foreign affairs, in more ways than one!'

'Oh?'

'Well, he had to go over to Brussels a lot,' Jane explained. 'He was reporting on the European Union. He flew over there for a few days once a month.'

Annie moved uncomfortably in her seat.

'Well, I found out eventually that he was having an affair with a woman over there,' she said. Annie noticed that there were tears in Jane's eyes as she continued, 'And, can you believe it, it had been going on for over a year before I found out.'

Jane looked at Annie as if asking for sympathy.

'How terrible for you,' said Annie, who was able to produce sympathy on demand.

'Yes!' said Jane, hitting her fist hard on the little table. Annie noticed that her fingers were white. 'Eight years we were together, and then I found out that he was having an affair with that . . . woman!'

Annie was more than a little surprised by the rise in emotional temperature. Jane seemed to have hidden depths.

'He told me he was going to Brussels for work,' Jane continued, 'but he forgot some papers he was working on. I rang his office and they said that he'd gone on holiday for a few days.'

'And did you ever find out who it was?' asked Annie, cautiously.

'Some English woman living in Brussels. God, if I'd found out her name, I'd have killed her!' said Jane. As she said this, she screwed up the empty plastic espresso cup with her plump hand, leaving it broken on the little table that separated her from Annie.

'So what did you do?' asked Annie, trying not to stare at the cup.

'I left him of course,' she said. 'I had to, I couldn't live with him any more . . . though I loved him, you know, loved him more than anything.' As she said 'loved', the tears that had formed in Jane's eyes a few moments before began to fall down her cheeks.

Annie looked at the teardrops almost in amazement. They were large and perfectly formed, just like a child's. She said nothing, but waited for the woman to stop crying.

'Silly me,' said Jane suddenly, wiping the tears away with the back of her hand and smiling weakly. 'It's so long ago.'

Suddenly the train slowed down; it was approaching a

station. Jane jumped up. 'Oh, this is Vernio already,' she said. 'I'd better get my bags.'

'Well, listen' said Annie brightly. 'It was wonderful to see you after all this time.' She was so relieved to see Jane go that she could hardly contain herself.

'Yes,' said Jane. 'Look, here's my address in case you're ever back in Italy and you want to come to Padova.' Jane took out a card from her handbag and gave it to Annie. Then she looked at Annie expectantly. Annie placed Jane's card on the table in front of her, then pulled out her own card from her briefcase and gave it to Jane, more out of politeness than any real desire that they should stay in touch.

'Take care of yourself,' said Annie.

It was quite a small rural station and the train wouldn't stop long. Jane Thomson leant over and kissed Annie on the cheek in the same way that she had when they were at university together. It felt strange to Annie, this kiss – a sign of the closeness that no longer existed between them. She kissed her friend on the cheek and smiled.

'Bye Annie,' said Jane. Then she was gone.

Annie breathed deeply and then sat back for the rest of the journey to Bologna. She thought about seeing Jane Thomson after all these years, going over their conversation and Jane's story in her mind. She was obviously an unhappy woman. Then there was James, Jane's ex-husband. He was a very handsome man, tall and slim. He had an athlete's body, she remembered, with long legs and a broad chest; he'd been a swimmer at university. And he had the most amazing bright blue eyes.

Annie had gone to Brussels the year after she left

university. James had visited the city often and the two met again by accident, in a restaurant. They had liked each other a lot. He came over to Brussels every month for work, and they had started seeing each other. Of course they became lovers. It had been a nice way to spend her fifteen months abroad, though it wasn't serious, just a bit of fun. It wasn't as if he was the only one. She couldn't remember very much about him now. Such a pity that Jane had found out! Their affair had lasted for a year and she had never seen him again.

Annie breathed heavily. In a few moments the train would pull into Bologna Centrale and she would start the next leg of her successful tour of Italy. That was the important thing, she told herself. The here and now. People worried so much about unimportant things. What did it matter who you had affairs with? No, she would never understand why people took these things so seriously. 'Aagh,' she said out loud and shook her head.

Annie started to collect her things. Jane Thomson's card still lay on the little table in front of her. 'Jane Thomson, City of Padova Museum' it said in plain black letters. Plain and black. That described her well, thought Annie, plain with black hair. Annie turned the card over in her fingers and saw that there was handwriting on the back. Annie stared at the small, child-like letters that read: 'I know it was you. And now I know where you live.'

That was all it said, but as Annie looked at the screwed up plastic coffee cup in front of her, she realised that it was enough.

Just the Facts

'The thing is, kid, you're there to record the facts,' said Gretzky. 'You always have to remember that. That's your job. Leave the morals to the politicians.' He laughed that laugh he had. A 'yack, yack, yack' laugh. A kind of Fred Flintstone laugh.

I didn't say anything.

'Facts, facts, facts . . . you know,' said Gretzky, clearing his throat to put on his 'official' voice. '"The prisoner's last meal request was two double meat cheeseburgers (all the way with mayonnaise and mustard), fries, fried chicken (well done), chocolate cake, a large vanilla ice cream, and six cans of cola." That's the kind of thing Joe Public wants to know,' he said. 'It sells newspapers and it doesn't hurt anyone.'

Gretzky paused for breath, and I took the opportunity to look out of the window at the passing countryside either side of highway US-190, the road from Livingston to Huntsville. It was four o'clock on an August afternoon and the heat was just beginning to die down. We were on our way to an execution – to watch a man being put to death for murder. The execution was timed for six.

The peace didn't last long. 'And, more important than all that, kid,' Gretzky took his right hand off the steering wheel and waved his finger in my face, 'is the fact that it keeps Jackson out of our hair.'

Len Jackson was the editor of the *Livingston Gazette*. I

hadn't known him for long, but I could see what Gretzky meant. He was a nice enough guy, and a good editor, but keeping him out of our hair seemed like a very good idea.

I'd just started as a junior reporter at the *Gazette* a month before. Tell you the truth, the job wasn't my first choice. But I was fresh out of college, and junior reporter jobs were hard to come by. And I needed work really badly. My dad had died a few years ago; Mom had given up a lot to put me through college and I couldn't take any more money from her. So here I was in Texas. My friends were amazed. 'Wow, Lisa, Texas!' they said. 'It's so different from Seattle.' Well, there was no denying that. It was a hell of a lot different. For one thing, it didn't rain as much.

The guy I worked with most at the *Livingston Gazette* was Ron Gretzky. Gretzky was the senior reporter. He was around fifty-five and thirty pounds overweight, almost the typical image of the hardened journalist. He'd seen it all, twice. He was never going to make editor; he just wasn't motivated or talented enough. For Gretzky, the years ahead to retirement meant more of the same. 'The three Ms, kid: marriages, muggings and murder, that's what this job's about,' he liked to say. 'Oh, yeah?' I'd joke with him. 'And what about the executions?' In the twenty years he'd been at the *Gazette*, he'd covered over three hundred executions. And if that isn't enough to harden a man, I don't know what is.

Now Gretzky was driving me to see my first execution. 'Best to take her this first time, Ron,' Len Jackson told him. 'Show her how it goes. Hold her hand, if you know what I mean.' Jackson had looked at me like he thought I might need help; after all I am a woman. And a young one at that. The idea was that, after this first one, I would cover executions on my own. Gretzky would move over. Maybe Jackson reckoned that Gretzky had done enough, that it was beginning to affect him. Way too late for that, was my feeling.

'Yeah, kid,' said Gretzky, still pointing his finger, 'just remember what these guys have done. They're criminals.'

There was a pause as Gretzky took one hand off the steering wheel, unwrapped the hamburger he'd brought for the journey and started eating. It gave me time to think about Gary Pearson, the guy who was going to lose his life today. I'd met him for the first time about three weeks ago on death row. They always let the media in to talk to the guy who's going to be executed a few weeks before the set date. 'You can do this alone, kid,' said Gretzky. 'It's good practice.' So I went along and waited nervously in line with the guys from the *Huntsville Echo* and Associated Press. Finally, it was my turn, and I got about forty-five minutes with Pearson.

Gary Pearson was a black guy from Houston. They said he was a burglar who went crazy one day and shot a judge. The story went that Pearson was breaking into the judge's house in a good neighbourhood of the city. The judge was at home and surprised Pearson. 'I didn't do it,' Pearson told me calmly. Gretzky had warned me that people on death row often told journalists they weren't guilty. I didn't say anything and concentrated on not showing any emotion. 'I was unlucky that the guy was a judge,' Pearson continued, 'and unlucky I was black.'

Yeah, unlucky as it turned out. The average length of time spent on death row is ten and a half years, and

Pearson had served about that. He was seventeen years old when the crime happened. I'd read that in most countries he would be considered a minor, under age, too young to be executed, but not here. I tried to put this uncomfortable fact out of my mind. But it is a fact.

'So, if you didn't do it,' I said, 'who did?'

'I don't know,' he said. 'I really don't know. The only thing I can tell you is that it wasn't me. I broke into the house, and disturbed the old guy, but when I left he was alive. I swear it.'

'But . . .'

'The police picked me up an hour or so later,' explained Pearson. 'I had some stuff from Judge Baker's house and the judge was dead. Who killed him? It had to be me.'

We talked some more. Pearson was calm and unemotional. 'Yes ma'am,' he said, when I commented on his coolness. 'I guess ten and a half years gives you enough time to come to terms with the idea that you're gonna die.'

He sighed.

'I've been through it all,' he went on. 'I've done a lot of crying, ma'am. I've done the begging and even the fighting. Seems like now I'm kinda resigned.' He sighed again. 'I don't have much confidence in the appeals any more. I guess it's time to die.'

'But,' I said at the end of the interview, 'you say you didn't do it. If that's really true, you have to fight!'

He just looked straight at me with a kind of soft, intelligent look and said, 'Believe me, ma'am, they're gonna kill me for this. It don't matter what the truth is.'

When Gretzky came to pick me up after the interview I

35

was so shaken that he had to take me for a drink. 'Happens to all of us the first time, kid,' he said, as we sat drinking bourbon in a bar in downtown Livingston. 'Soon it'll be just like any other job to you.'

'But he says he didn't do it, Ron,' I said, my hands still shaking as I drank the strong liquor, 'and he sounds like he's telling the truth.'

Gretzky shook his head. 'They always do, kid, they always do. And remember that you're a young woman . . . He was just looking for sympathy.'

It was true what Gretzky said. Guys on death row often tell you they're innocent. What have they got to lose? But anyway, there were a lot of doubts in my mind after talking to Pearson, and they came out in my story. I showed it to Gretzky. He coughed and coffee went everywhere.

'Want my advice, kid? he said, 'Go back and write this again! Jackson's just gonna throw it at you. "Is Pearson innocent?" Ah! Are you *trying* to lose your job?'

'But what about the truth?'

'Truth?' Gretzky laughed. 'You think that you know what the truth is, kid? That's a *sure* way to end up on the street!'

So, in the end, I wrote a story which didn't really say anything much. I was scared of Jackson, scared of losing my job. And anyway Gretzky could be right. I felt pretty bad, but I figured that if I really wanted a career as a journalist, I'd have to make a name for myself before I could write what I really thought.

And now here I was on my way to see Pearson put to death. I wondered if he had already eaten his last meal. They said that it was only a guilty man who ordered a big meal; if a man was innocent he probably wouldn't eat at all.

Gretzky finished the hamburger and wiped his mouth with the back of his hand. 'Think of the victim,' he growled, 'and think of the victim's family. Gonna stop at this gas station, kid. We need some gas, and I need the bathroom.'

Gretzky pulled the Buick up to the pump at the Exxon gas station. A young guy with long thin black hair came to fill the tank. Gretzky got out of the car and went towards the bathroom at the side of the building. I turned the car radio on low.

Think of the victim and the family, Gretzky had said. I'd read somewhere that the victim's family often wants the guy who's being executed to suffer more. A lethal injection they said, killed the guy too quickly. The judge's wife had died twenty years ago but there was a son, John, and a daughter, Kathy.

Like his father, John Baker was a lawyer. In fact he was one of the top lawyers in Houston and a powerful kinda guy. He had made sure that his father's killer was found guilty. Baker was always on TV talking about how important it was to get justice and he was determined to see Pearson executed. He would sit there today, behind the glass in one of the viewing rooms, and, like me, see a man be put to death. I wondered about Kathy Baker. Nobody had seen her for a very long time. They said she'd gone to live in Europe. No journalist had ever got near her.

I took the information sheet for reporters out of my jacket pocket. 'Drugs used in the lethal injection,' it said, 'are Sodium Thiopental (puts a person to sleep),

Pancuronium Bromide (muscle relaxant – collapses lungs), Potassium Chloride (stops heart beat). The prisoner is usually pronounced dead approximately seven minutes after the lethal injection begins. The cost of each execution for drugs used is $86.08.' What would it feel like, seeing eighty-six dollars worth of drugs being injected into a guy, putting him to sleep forever?

Gretzky arrived back from the bathroom, still adjusting the belt of his trousers. 'What ya reading?' he asked, looking at the information sheet. 'Ah yeah . . . But you're lucky, kid. It's so much cleaner than when they used to kill 'em with an electric shock.

'Oh good,' I said. 'I like clean.'

'Not that I ever saw anyone die from an electric shock.' Gretzky went on, ignoring the comment. 'It was before my time. But you can only imagine.'

I tried not to imagine. It was bad enough thinking about the lethal injection. 'So, what's it like seeing a man tied to a bed and killed, just ten feet away from you?' I asked Gretzky.

'Well,' he said, settling himself behind the steering wheel and putting on his seat belt, 'it's like a ceremony, kid. It's hard to explain. It's not really very emotional. You'll be fine.

'Anyway,' he went on, 'it's not killing, kid. It's *execution*. Killing is what *he* did, this Pearson.'

Oh yeah. Sometimes I found it hard to see the difference.

'Isn't killing always killing?' I asked Gretzky. At times I couldn't help myself.

'Well now, kid,' Gretzky said, 'that's way too

philosophical. The guy's gone out and killed a man. No one made him do it; he has to take responsibility for that.'

Gretzky reached to start the engine. Suddenly, the back door of the Buick opened and someone jumped into the back seat. Shocked by the sudden movement, I turned around and was even more shocked to see a slim young woman, dressed in a pale blue T-shirt and jeans. She was maybe twenty-eight, twenty-nine. She'd come from nowhere. She looked kinda familiar.

'Face the front,' the woman said to me. Then she said to Gretzky, 'And you drive. Don't try anything or I'll blow your brains out.' She had a slight Texan accent. She didn't shout, but she sounded like she meant business.

I had noticed that the woman was holding both her hands low down so that they couldn't be seen through the car window. She could easily have a gun.

'Come on.' she said to Gretzky. 'Move!' The woman sounded nervous and I hoped that Gretzky would do what he was told.

There was a moment when nothing seemed to happen; it hung in the air for what felt like hours. I looked at Gretzky out of the corner of my eye and hoped that he would start the car. Finally, Gretzky started the engine and steered the Buick slowly out of the gas station. 'Where am I going?' he said, his voice hardly more than a whisper.

'Towards Huntsville.'

Gretzky got back on US-190 and we headed towards Huntsville again. I glanced at Gretzky. His round face, usually pink, had gone a greyish white.

I was still trying to figure out why the woman was so familiar to me. I closed my eyes and tried to remember her face, which I'd seen so briefly. I thought about her short brown hair and almost boyish build. Suddenly I had a flash of a news program I'd seen a few months ago, before I'd even started working at the *Gazette*. The program was about the Judge Baker murder and they'd shown an old college photo of Kathy Baker, his daughter. But that was practically the last anyone had seen of her. Could the woman with the gun sitting in the back seat of the Buick be Kathy Baker?

In a few moments I had my answer.

'I read your article, Miss Thomas,' said the woman, 'the one about Pearson.'

There was a brief silence.

'It was garbage,' she said.

'I, er . . .'

'Gary Pearson didn't kill my father,' said Kathy Baker, clearly and firmly, 'and I'm sure that Pearson told you that.'

'But they always tell us that!' said Gretzky.

'Shut up, Gretzky,' said the woman. 'There's a lot to say and do, and we haven't got much time. Turn the radio up, Miss Thomas. That's the news.'

Well, Kathy Baker certainly knew who we were. I turned the car radio up, just in time to hear the news. It was five o'clock. An hour to go before the execution.

'In exactly one hour's time,' said the newsreader, 'Gary Pearson will be executed for the murder of Judge William A. Baker . . .'

'Garbage!' said Kathy Baker.

'So Pearson didn't kill your father?' I asked her.

'Of course he didn't!' the judge's daughter answered.

'How do I know that?' she shouted. 'Because, Miss Thomas, I killed him!'

I didn't say anything but I heard Gretzky breathing fast.

'Oh, I know what you're thinking,' she said. 'You think I'm crazy! Oh no, I'm not crazy. Shhh! Listen!'

'The dead judge's son, John Baker,' the voice on the radio went on, 'spoke this morning to HBC Radio.'

Then came John Baker's voice, clear and firm: 'This is the day we've all been waiting for,' he said, 'the day when the man who killed my father finally gets what he deserves.'

'Ah,' said Kathy Baker, 'my brother is always so convincing!'

The next news item came on and I turned the radio off.

'You killed him?' I turned to Kathy Baker.

'Listen carefully, Miss Thomas,' said Kathy Baker, 'because God knows what's going to happen, and I want you to be able to tell my story.'

We were just two kilometers from the Huntsville Unit, the place where the execution would take place.

'Go ahead,' I said.

'Well,' she began, 'the truth is that my father was a terrible man, a bully. He used to shout and hit my mother and me every day. His bullying frightened us so much that we did whatever he wanted. It's the same old story. Everyone thought he was wonderful, a good judge and "the heart and soul of the community." And to the outside world he looked like that. But the fact is that he was a dreadful man. He killed my mother with his bullying, just the same as if he had taken a gun and shot her.' Kathy Baker's voice got soft and it sounded like she was going to

41

cry. 'I watched it happen,' she went on. 'He bullied both of us every single day. I hated him!'

'And your brother . . . What about John?'

'Ah, my dear brother!' said Kathy. 'My brother saw it all, but my father never bullied him in the same way. John loved my father very much and made excuses for everything he did. John's story is that my mother and I asked for it, that somehow it wasn't his fault.'

I looked at Gretzky's grey face staring straight ahead at the road.

Kathy Baker sighed deeply and continued her story. 'My father kept guns,' she said, 'like most folk around here. He kept them in his study. Oh, I knew where they were; I'd known all my life.' Kathy Baker spoke fast; she was eager to tell her story, as if no one had ever listened before. 'He had some valuable things in his study too, some paintings and such.'

'I was nineteen years old, in my first year at college,' she went on, 'That evening – it was a Friday – my father was in his study, drinking as usual. He drank whiskey, and by nine o'clock he was always drunk. At about eleven thirty I went to bed, leaving my father asleep with his head on the desk in his study. He was dead drunk and I couldn't move him. So I left him there, asleep, and turned the lights out. It wasn't the first time I'd left him like that.'

'I went upstairs to bed,' she continued. 'I fell asleep very quickly and was woken up about two hours later by my father shouting. He was still in his study on the ground floor. Someone had got in through one of the small windows that he'd left open. The burglar had started looking for things to take and walked into my father. My father woke up and started shouting and swearing at the top of his voice.'

'So you went down?'

She nodded. 'I ran downstairs, to see the burglar running down the street with some of my father's things under his arm.'

There was a brief pause in her story as she remembered that scene so long ago.

'My father turned on me,' Kathy said. 'He started hitting me and shouting, swearing, blaming me for leaving the window open. It was really terrible. My father was a very big man.'

I remembered seeing photographs of the judge on the TV program where I'd first seen the picture of Kathy. He really was very tall and well-built and Kathy Baker was small and slim.

'Then, in his drunken state, he tried to . . . you know . . . just like he used to with my mother. I fought him off and he hit me.'

Kathy Baker paused again.

'He hit me so hard,' she went on, 'that I fell against the cupboard where the guns were. I knew which guns had bullets in. I took one of them out of the cupboard and pointed it at him. I didn't really mean to shoot him, but he just kept coming towards me. He was drunk and smelled of liquor. I thought about my mother and all the times he'd left her bruised and crying. Then I thought about myself. I shot him twice through the head.'

Kathy Baker took a deep breath. I looked at Gretzky but he was just staring ahead at the road, his large, round face now dripping with sweat.

'And no one heard the shot?' I asked.

'No,' said the young woman. 'Our house was well away from any other houses. Anything could happen there, and no one would ever know.'

Yes, I thought, that was how Judge Baker had managed to abuse his wife and family for so long.

'I was very upset, hysterical,' she went on. 'I called my brother and told him the whole story, told him what had happened.'

'And . . .?'

'I told him about the burglar,' Kathy Baker explained, 'and how my father had turned on me. When John heard about the burglar, that he was a black kid, he just said, "Don't worry, Kathy. There's a way of working this out."'

'He made up a story?' I asked.

'Just like that,' she answered. 'The story was that my father had disturbed the black kid and that the kid had shot him. Pearson was picked up later that night with stuff from the house, and he was charged with murder.'

'But the gun . . .?' I asked.

'John fixed it all,' she said. 'Wiped my fingerprints off the handle and somehow managed to get Pearson's on there. My brother is a very powerful man, with powerful friends. Everybody believed it.'

'And what about you?' I asked.

Kathy Baker sighed deeply. 'This is the worst part. I . . . I agreed to it, Miss Thomas,' she said. 'Oh, at first I wanted to tell the truth. After all, it was self-defence. But my brother said that they'd never believe me, that I'd go to prison; in this state they might even execute me. After all, my father was respected in the community. My brother is a persuasive and powerful man. I was a kid; I was scared to death! I've been scared to death all these years.'

'So your brother sent you to Europe?' I asked.

'He said it was for the best,' said Kathy, 'and I believed him.'

'And so Gary Pearson is losing his life . . .'

'. . . for something he never did.' Kathy Baker finished my sentence and added, 'And it's only now that I've got the courage to come forward.'

It certainly was late, I thought, perhaps too late. I looked out of the window and saw a sign for the Huntsville Unit. I looked ahead and saw the low building ahead of us beside the road. We didn't have much time.

'How did you find us?'

'Well, I had your names,' she said, 'and I saw Gretzky on TV, talking about all the executions he's been to. I knew which newspaper you worked for and I found out which car you drove. I knew you'd be going to the execution, so I just waited . . .'

'But what if we hadn't stopped here?'

'It was a chance I had to take,' she said. 'But it's the only gas station on this road. Otherwise, I don't know . . . I guess I would have stood on the road and waved you down.'

Suddenly Gretzky slowed down. We were at the Unit; in front of us there were police officers and cars. Behind them I could see John Baker, a look of surprise on his face as he saw his sister.

Kathy Baker got out of the back of the car. I looked at her, expecting to see a gun, but she didn't have one. She ran up to the police officers and said, 'I would like to say that

Gary Pearson did not kill my father, Judge William A. Baker. He is innocent. *I* killed my father.

'And he knows it!' she added, pointing at her brother.

'She's telling the truth!' I shouted. As soon as I'd said it, I knew I was right: she *was* telling the truth. The policemen just stared at me.

'She's telling the truth,' I said again. I felt like I was talking in a dream, one of those dreams where you're trying to speak, but no one can hear you. 'Gretzky, tell them!'

Gretzky held up his hands and said, 'Well now, kid, come on . . . How can you be sure she's telling the truth?'

'Gretzky!' I screamed, but he just looked at me. I turned away from him in disgust. Up until then I'd thought he was lazy but harmless. Now I knew that he was the kind of self-satisfied man who turns away from injustice because it is just too uncomfortable to do anything about it.

I ran towards John Baker. 'You've got to stop this execution,' I said, trying to keep my voice calm.

Baker looked at me and said, 'My sister is obviously very ill.' His face was expressionless. He turned towards one of the police officers and said, 'Perhaps you should take her away.' They took Kathy Baker away in a car, struggling and shouting.

'Where's Pearson's lawyer?' I shouted at no one in particular. 'I demand to see Pearson's lawyer!'

'It's too late for that, ma'am,' said one of the police officers. 'The execution's about to happen, and everyone has to go in.'

John Baker walked towards the building where the execution would take place. I ran after him, shouting desperately, 'Too late! How can it be too late? This is a man's life!'

I was running, but I wasn't getting anywhere. It was like one of those dreams where you can't move. Like you're running through mud. I ran past the police officers and managed to get through the door. But I didn't get far. After just a few meters I felt two officers holding me by the arms. They pulled me back and took me outside again.

I remembered what Pearson had said when I saw him: 'Believe me, ma'am, they're gonna kill me for this. It don't matter what the truth is.'

Gretzky and everyone else turned to go into the place of execution. The door closed. There was no one left. All I could do was cry into the warm air of a Texan summer evening as they executed Gary Pearson.

*   *   *

I carried on running. I ran as long and as hard as I could. I ran away from the place where they could execute a man for something he hadn't done. I ran from the place where they could execute men at all.

I ran from the place where I would become the kind of journalist I hated, the kind that could no longer recognise the truth. Where I would become like Gretzky, weak and lazy. Where I would become the kind of person who lets injustice happen because they don't speak out.

I ran all the way back to Seattle. I had no money and no chance of getting the kind of job I wanted, but at least I could live with myself. I got a job waiting on tables in a diner so I didn't have to take money from my mother. At last I found a little newspaper where the editor would let me write my story, let me tell my truth.

I wrote my article and told the story of how Gary Pearson was a kid of seventeen from the poor side of town who burgled rich houses. Of how they tried him for a murder he never committed. I wrote the story of the judge who everyone thought was a respectable man in the community but who was a bully and a drunk. I wrote the story of the daughter he had abused, who had killed him out of self-defence and was then too scared to tell what really happened and the story of how Kathy Baker had finally tried to tell the truth, but wasn't allowed to.

I wrote the story of how power can do anything, even execute an innocent man.

I wrote the facts. Just the facts.

Water in the Desert

The desert was dark pink, the sky was baby blue; the whole thing looked good enough to eat. The road from Santa Fe made its way like a black snake through the red and pink landscape. Through the hot air the tall man standing at the side of the road could see the sharp mountain peaks of the Rockies in the distance.

At last a truck came. The first thing he heard was the distant sound of an engine. Sweetest sound in the whole world when you've been out in the desert sun for two hours and you're beginning to think you might die there. Real sweet. He blinked at the road and looked ahead, listening. Yeah, it was a truck alright.

He ran up through the bushes at the side of the road and stood right there staring into the distance, so that he could see the truck as soon it came into view. Then he saw it, a bright piece of silver, with sunlight bouncing off it in all directions. A great silver insect crawling across the stillness of the desert floor of New Mexico.

As the truck got nearer he tried to make out the driver. Looked like a woman. A woman with dark red hair and sunglasses, those kind of shades that the sun bounces off too. Well, that was that, he thought. No way was a woman alone going to stop for a guy hitchhiking in the middle of nowhere. He turned away. The truck just rolled on, just like he knew it would.

But then he heard the sound of brakes as the truck came

to a stop about two hundred meters further on. He turned around again and looked at the clouds of dust the truck had thrown up. After a minute or so the dust settled, the door of the driver's cab swung open and a pair of blue jeans came down from the cab. The woman appeared, wearing a white 'cowgirl' shirt and western boots to go with the jeans. She still had her sunglasses on. The man wondered whether her eyes were green. He always did like green eyes.

He walked slowly towards the truck. 'Can I help you, ma'am?' he asked, trying to see her eyes behind the shades.

She looked at him long and hard, like she was trying to work out if he was dangerous. The man did his best to look harmless.

'Yeah, well . . . looks like my brakes froze up,' she said. '. . . a rock must have cut the brake pipe.' She paused, and must have decided that he seemed OK because she said, 'You any good with tape?'

'You got any?' he asked.

'There's some in the back of the cab,' she said. 'I'll get it.'

She got back into the cab and came back a few minutes later with the tape. He took it and crawled under the truck.

'How's it going?' she shouted after a few minutes.

'Hot as hell!' he shouted back.

About ten minutes later he found the place where the air line had been cut. 'Here it is!' he shouted. 'A big fat hole the size of Texas.' He set to work taping it, and crawled back out some time later, hot and dirty. The woman was still standing there in the full heat of the sun.

'That should do it,' the man said to her. 'How far you gonna go?'

'Denver,' she said, moving towards the cab.

'Denver? Me too. But I guess . . .'

She looked at him again, up and down. 'Get in,' she said slowly. 'You look pretty harmless to me and I guess I owe you something.'

'Hey,' he said, 'thanks.'

'Yeah,' she said. They both got into the driver's cab. Even with the air conditioning off, it was cool, at least a hell of a lot cooler than outside.

'Have some water,' she said. 'What ya doing out here anyway? You crazy?' She passed him a water bottle and he drank. The water was sweet and cool. He drank thirstily, letting it run down the sides of his mouth and onto his neck. He didn't answer her.

'So?' she asked again.

'Well, it's a long story . . .' he said.

She pushed up her glasses to take a proper look and flashed a smile at him. She had the whitest teeth he'd ever seen. And she did have the prettiest green eyes. 'Yeah, well save it for later; it's going to be a long trip,' she said, still smiling. And with that she put her glasses down and started the engine up again.

The truck continued its journey through the high flat desert that makes up most of I-25, the main highway from New Mexico to Colorado. As she drove, the man looked at her hands on the wheel. Small, strong hands. He couldn't stop looking at the New Mexican turquoise ring she was wearing. The colour was so beautiful. Kind of held your attention. After a while the ring and the endlessness of the desert made him feel light-headed. Perhaps he'd been out in the sun for too long.

'You got anything to eat in here?' he asked her. 'All that work made me kinda hungry.'

'Sure.' She smiled at him, a flash of green eyes. 'Have a look in the cooler.' He opened it, found a piece of bread and some cheese and ate hungrily. They rode along in silence for a while. He stared out of the window at the desert.

'You got a name?' she asked suddenly.

'Sure, my name's Ted,' he said. 'How about you?'

'Lee,' she said.

'That's a pretty name,' he said. 'Pleased to meet you.'

There was another half-hour of silence as the truck made its way across the desert floor.

'I can't help but notice that you ain't got any luggage Ted,' she said suddenly.

'That's right,' he said. 'I left it in Denver with some friends. I'm gonna pick it up when I get there. 'Have you been driving trucks long?' he asked.

'Yeah, well, a couple of years,' she said.

'Like it?'

'It's a living.' She smiled that smile again and added, 'I love the scenery.' She nodded towards the window.

As the man followed her glance out into the bright sunlight he saw a sign coming towards them at the side of the road. 'Do not pick up hitchhikers,' said the sign. He glanced at her. If she had seen it she wasn't going to say anything. That was just fine by him, he thought.

'Yeah, it is pretty,' he said.

He closed his eyes. Very soon he fell asleep. He woke up to the truck coming to a stop outside a gas station. The noise of the brakes and the sudden movement made him jump.

'Hey,' said Lee, laughing. 'Coming back to life, eh?'

He rubbed his eyes and looked around. The sun had lost some of its fierceness. He guessed it was around five. There were two other trucks parked at the gas station and in the diner next to it he could see the drivers drinking coffee and eating hamburgers.

'I'm just going to freshen up,' she said.

She picked up her wash bag, went off to the drivers' rest room and came back a few minutes later. She'd combed her hair and looked really nice. 'You gonna get something to drink, Ted?' she asked.

'Ah no,' he said. 'I'm fine. I'll wait for you.'

'I'll just pick up a cola and a burger,' she said. 'Sure you don't want anything?'

'Well . . . that sounds good,' he said, changing his mind.

She came back a few minutes later with the drinks and burgers. Then she parked the truck round the back of the diner and they settled down to eat. The desert air was still hot and the ice-cold cola tasted great.

'So what did you do before you started driving trucks?' he asked her, between mouthfuls of burger.

'Oh, this and that,' she said. 'I worked as a ski instructor up in Aspen for a couple of years.'

'Hey!' he said, 'that must have been a great job. Did you meet lots of famous people?'

She laughed. 'Well yeah,' she said, 'lots . . . and it *was* a great job.'

'So why did you stop?' he asked.

'I had an accident,' she said, shaking her head. 'One day I was skiing downhill, really fast. The snow was great, the sun was wonderful. Everything was just fine, then bang! I fell and the next thing I knew I was in hospital.'

'It sounds bad,' he said.

'Well, could have been worse,' she continued. 'I ended up with just a broken leg and some bruised ribs but it took a few months to recover. When I was well, I decided that it was time for a change, time to do something new. You know what I mean?'

'Well, yeah, sometimes you just have to make changes,' he said, hardly knowing what he meant. There was something about this woman that made you want to talk to her, tell her about the secret places in your mind.

'Wow! Look at that!' she said suddenly, pointing towards the mountains in the distance. The huge sky had turned orange with the light from the dying sun; it looked like someone had lit a huge fire behind the mountains. Nature was giving them the full display and it was beautiful.

'That's what I mean,' she said. 'The scenery's just to die for. Worth more than all the money in the world.'

They finished their colas and left, heading out towards the state border between New Mexico and Colorado.

'Truth is,' she started almost as soon as they started off again, 'I was trying to get away from a guy. I mean . . . that's why I got out of Aspen.'

'Oh really?'

'Yeah,' she said, laughing nervously. 'Well, he was my husband in fact. I'd been trying for years to get away from him. But I couldn't . . . Then I had this accident and I thought it was a good chance to disappear.' There was a pause. 'You don't mind me telling you all this, do you, Ted?'

'No, I don't,' he replied kindly. 'No way. But tell me, how did you get mixed up with him in the first place . . . if you don't mind me asking.'

She looked at him and sighed. 'Well . . . I met him when I was eighteen. He was twenty-one. That was back in my home town, Pueblo, Colorado. God, what a place that is! Ever been there?'

He shook his head.

'Lucky you!' she said. 'Home of the living dead, I swear. It's the kind of place you have to escape from. Anyway, he was the best-looking guy in Pueblo, though that's not saying much.' She laughed. 'No, he was really cute, really nice. We got married when I was nineteen.'

'That sure is young,' he said.

'I guess I didn't know any better,' she carried on. 'And anything was better than living at home, let me tell you. Anyway, it was the same old story. Before we got married he was the sweetest guy in the world. Brought me flowers, presents. Treated me nice, you know. I'd never met a man who could be that nice. But then things changed.'

'Changed?'

'Yeah, well he changed practically overnight,' she said. 'Soon after we got married he started drinking a lot, going out with his friends. He never took me out any more.'

'And?'

'Well, I would do something small, something kinda insignificant like making too much noise, but it would be enough to make him get violent,' she said. 'You know, it was like an excuse . . .'

'He hit you?' he asked.

'He did, and I got the scars to prove it!' she replied.

'When he drank he just couldn't control himself. And he drank a lot. A real whiskey drinker. Then he started gambling and going with other women.'

'And that was as soon as you got married?' he asked.

'Yeah, and it got worse,' she answered. 'My friends told me he had other women, but I knew that – it was obvious. There were nights when he just didn't come home. When he finally turned up in the morning you could smell the whiskey and the women on him.'

'So . . .?'

'Why did he want to stay with me?' She asked the question for him. 'He just couldn't live without me. Oh, he had his women, but he always came back. He needed someone to push around, to make him feel like a man.' She shook her head. 'I used to pray that he'd drop dead or find someone else and stay away from me. I swear I had seven years of hell!'

'Seven years?' he said, shocked. 'You put up with that for seven years?'

'Oh, it's not like I didn't try to get out,' she said. 'Almost every single day, believe me. But it was like being in jail. No matter how sweet the grass smells outside your cell, you just can't get free.'

'Er . . . yeah,' he said.

'I tried everything,' she continued. 'Left in the middle of the night, changed states, changed my name. Somehow he always found me! That's why I decided to leave Aspen after the accident. I knew that it was only a matter of time before he found me again.' She shivered, remembering the fear.

Lee stopped talking for a moment as she struggled with

her feelings. They both listened to the silence of the desert, only broken by the comforting noise of the engine. Then she spoke again, this time in a softer voice.

'I'd loved him, you know, I mean in the beginning.' she said. 'Yeah, loved him. But then it all changed for me. I started to hate him.' Then she added seriously, 'Matter of fact, that's the worse thing about it all. You learn about hate; you discover that you can hate somebody that much. You lose your innocence, you know?'

He nodded. He knew what she meant.

'I was a kid when I met him,' she continued. 'I was so full of dreams. I thought the world was full of love. That I was full of love . . . He taught me a lesson alright, taught me how to hate, just like everyone else.' She took a deep breath. 'It takes time to get over that,' she said. 'It takes time to find love again. Even to find it in your own heart.'

She sighed and went quiet. Her face looked kind of sad.

'So what happened?' he asked after a few minutes. 'I mean, where is he now?'

'Ha!' she said loudly. 'He finally got it! Finally got what he deserved! Got killed in a bar one night in Taos.'

'In Taos?'

'Yeah, got into a fight with some guy,' she answered. 'Over a woman, of course. Anyway, the guy shot him, cool as you like. The police called in the middle of the night to tell me the bad news. I swear, Ted, I could hardly keep the smile off my face. First thought that came into my head was, "I'm free! I've been in jail and now I'm free!" I just went away and tried to forget.' She smiled now, remembering it all. 'Don't know why I'm telling you all this,' she added.

57

There was silence for a while, apart from the soft murmur of the engine. They were about an hour from the border with Colorado. It was evening now; the softening light wrapped around them like a blanket.

After about twenty minutes, she said, 'Let's get over Raton Pass and into Colorado, then we can catch some sleep.'

'Great idea,' he said. They were still another seven hours or so from Denver.

'Mind if I turn on the radio?' she asked.

'Er . . . no,' he said, 'how about a music channel?'

'Sure,' she said and turned it on. It was Anita Baker singing 'Giving you the best that I've got.'

The man closed his eyes and listened to her sweet voice. It was like honey pouring into the truck. Lee started singing along to the radio.

'Mmm . . . pretty voice,' he said.

Lee didn't say anything, but carried on singing.

The song ended. Then a man's voice came over the radio: 'And now it's eight thirty and on Radio New Mexico we have some news for you, so let's go over to the newsroom and Chucho Martinez.'

The man cleared his throat. 'Er, why don't we change channel and get some more music?' he said.

'Shh,' said Lee. 'In a minute. Let me hear the news.'

He kept his eyes closed. 'Good evening, and the news tonight is that a man has escaped from the New Mexico State Prison just outside Santa Fe. The man is Jed King, doing life for killing twenty-eight-year-old Tony García in a bar fight in Taos, New Mexico, four years ago. Drivers are being warned by the state police tonight not to pick up hitchhikers. And that's particularly if you're driving on I-25. And now on to other news . . .'

He still kept his eyes firmly closed.

'Well,' said Lee suddenly, turning off the radio, 'we're almost there. There's Raton Pass just ahead of us.'

The man opened his eyes a little and looked up towards the pass. It was the time just before darkness falls; in another fifteen or twenty minutes the light would be completely gone. Right now the sky was an incredible red and purple, the day's last light show. The truck started to climb towards the top of the pass. He closed his eyes again.

They drove along in silence as they reached the top and started down the other side of the pass. He kept his eyes shut like he was asleep, but his mind was racing. He thought back to that night in Taos. The night he killed Tony García.

'You're him, aren't you?'

The man jumped.

'You're Jed King, the man who killed Tony . . . the man who killed my husband,' she said. Her voice was low. 'You've escaped from jail.'

He opened his eyes a little and nodded.

'I never went to the trial,' she said. 'Tell you the truth, I never thought about who killed him. I was just happy he was gone.'

He looked across at her. She looked calm, kind of peaceful somehow.

They had reached the other side of the pass and had already crossed the state border some time back. Lee turned the wheel and pulled the truck off the road. They were surrounded by darkness, parked in a rest area well away from the lights of the highway. She turned to look at him and he could just make out her face, her bright green eyes shining. Like cat's eyes on a dark road.

'That's right,' he said. 'I killed him. But I swear it was self-defence. I didn't mean to . . .'

As he said it, unbelievably, he started to cry. He hadn't cried for a long time, maybe since he was a kid. 'I didn't mean to . . . I didn't mean to . . .' He was actually weeping, great sobs coming from his chest.

It was like some kind of wall breaking. Suddenly Jed King felt the full force of the injustice of it all, a feeling he hadn't allowed himself to have before. He remembered the trial, with the jury who didn't believe his story, and the 'witnesses', García's friends, who had lied in court. He remembered the moment when the judge had said the words, 'You will go to jail for life.' He cried for the four years he had been locked up in the hell of the state penitentiary because he had killed a man who otherwise would have killed him. He cried at the feeling that he would never again be really free, never be able to listen to the silence of the desert or see the sun set over the mountains without being afraid. 'It wasn't my fault, believe me. You have to believe me!' he said. 'I never wanted to . . .'

She leaned over towards him and put her finger on his lips. 'Shhh,' she said, running her fingers around his mouth. 'I know, I know,' she said, softly. 'It sounds like we both escaped from a life sentence.' Then she kissed him.

They lay on the little bed just behind the cab and looked at the night sky through the little window in the roof. It was dark blue with a pattern of stars, like something from a child's storybook. The desert moon was so big you could see its dark and light areas. It was very cold now, in that way the desert has of suddenly showing you that it knows how to do both.

It takes time, she had said, to find love again, even to find it in your own heart. As they lay there in the stillness of the desert, he knew that they had both found a way back to love, a way back from despair. Somehow he knew that it would all come right. He would be able to prove that he had shot García in self-defence. He had found hope.

But that was all for later. Right now they lay there in the moonlight. It was hard to describe the look they had on their faces as they listened to the silence. Perhaps you would call it relief. Yeah, that was it, relief. It was the look you have when you find something precious you thought you'd lost, the look you have when someone you've been waiting for shows up at last, the look you have when, after a long search, you find cool, sweet water in the desert.

The Knowledge

'Taxi!'

It was a cold dark night in central London. The rain was falling heavily. The black cab stopped just in front of the man in the hat and the black overcoat, splashing water everywhere. The driver leaned out of the window.

'Where're you going, mate? Chinatown? OK, get in; it'll be about ten pounds. It'll take about twenty, twenty-five minutes. There's a lot of traffic because of the rain. Terrible weather isn't it? It seems to have been raining for days. Well, it's been a bad year for weather altogether. Dreadful! Typical English weather, eh? Still, at least it's good for the farmers. Ha!

Chinatown eh? You know, it's a funny thing, but this all reminds me of a Chinese bloke I picked up from here going to Chinatown. Must have been November, about this time last year. It was raining then too, absolutely pouring down. He was a strange guy; it's a strange story – the strangest thing that's happened to me in all my years in a cab . . .

To tell you the truth, I really just wanted to go home. You know how it is. It was about half past ten on a Tuesday evening and I was going to call it a day. As I said, it was like this – cold, wet and miserable. I'd been working hard for months and I felt like I wanted to go home early for a change and see Marlene – that was my girlfriend.

But then I saw him, the Chinese bloke, I mean. He was

in his early thirties, I suppose. Thin, kind of hungry-looking. He was standing there, on George Street, where you were just now, and dripping wet just like you. That's why I say it reminds me. Well, I thought to myself, "I'll just pick this bloke up, then I'll go home."

So I leaned my head out of the cab window and into the rain. "Where are you going, mate?"

"Chinatown" said the bloke, and he told me the name of the street. It was Gerrard Street. Well, it'd only take me twenty, twenty-five minutes to get there, I thought. I could be home by eleven o'clock. That's early for me.

I took a really good look at him before he got in. He was wearing an old leather jacket and blue jeans. Not really dressed for the rain, you know. And he was carrying a parcel under his arm, wrapped in brown paper. He seemed in a bit of a hurry, but that wasn't surprising. Probably just wanted to get out of the rain, like everybody else. He looked OK; at least he wasn't drunk, so I said, "Fine, get in."

To be honest, I'm really careful about who I let in the back of my cab these days, especially when it's late at night. Have a good look at 'em, you know? Terrible things happen to taxi drivers. A friend of mine got hit over the head with a bottle. Ended up in hospital, poor devil. He picked up a bloke late one Saturday night outside a club in the West End. The bloke was drunk of course, I mean really drunk. Anyway, when they got wherever they were going, the bloke refused to pay his fare. When my friend said he would call the police, the drunk just took an empty bottle out of his pocket and hit him over the head. My friend had to spend the night in hospital. But he was lucky!

There are stories of taxi drivers being knifed, even shot. I tell you, mate, London is getting worse every day.

Anyway, back to this Chinese bloke. Well, he shook himself as he got in the back of the cab and said, "Phew! It's wet out there."

I laughed and looked at him in my mirror. He had straight black hair and it was stuck to his forehead like he'd been swimming. He looked kind of funny, you know.

"Live in Chinatown do you?" I asked, like you do. Just to make conversation really.

He didn't say anything for a few minutes. As a matter of fact I thought he hadn't understood me, but then suddenly he said, "Have you heard of Bruce Lee?"

"Of course I have!" I said. "Everybody's heard of Bruce Lee! He's really, really famous. I mean he was. And a fantastic fighter."

Well, Bruce Lee's the most famous martial artist of all time, isn't he? Kung fu and all that. I've got all the Bruce Lee films at home, bought them when I was a bit younger. To tell you the truth, I still watch them sometimes. Yeah, I sit down with a beer and watch my old kung fu films.

"*Enter the Dragon*'s my favourite," I said to the Chinese bloke. "Great film."

"Thank you," he said.

I laughed. It was a funny thing to say, you know, so I asked him, "What . . . did you direct it or something?"

"No," he said, "but I am Bruce Lee."

I had to laugh. "Oh yeah," I said, "and I'm Marilyn Monroe!"

"No, really, I am. I'm Bruce Lee," he said again.

Now it's a funny kind of job being a taxi driver, you

know? I've often thought that it's a bit like having an affair, like a holiday romance. I mean, you meet someone for a short time, and she can tell you anything and you can tell her anything. Know what I mean, mate? You're probably never going to see her again, so . . . Ha! Well, it's the same in the cab. I've heard some really wild stories, believe me. Like I picked up this guy who told me he'd just been hired to murder the head of the United Nations. Told me he was carrying a gun in his pocket. He frightened me to death, I can tell you. Then there was the woman who told me she was the Queen and she never carried money. So Bruce Lee was strange, but not that strange, if you know what I mean.

"Oh, Bruce Lee," I said, trying to sound normal, you know. "Er . . . I thought he was dead."

The man laughed. "Well, he isn't."

I took another look at the bloke in my mirror. Funny thing was, he did look a bit like Bruce Lee. Good-looking sort of man with really dark eyes.

"Yes, it's me," he said, smiling.

Funny thing was, when he said that, I almost believed him. Though you know and I know that Bruce Lee died years ago. Right, mate?

"Oh, so you've been training, then?" I asked him. Best thing was to go along with him, you know. We were still about twenty minutes away from Chinatown. For all I knew, he was totally crazy and had a gun in his pocket. That's the kind of thing you have to think of when you've got someone in the back of your cab.

"Yes," he said, "perfecting my one-inch punch."

Now, I remembered seeing a documentary about Bruce Lee a few years ago. Do you know that he could knock a man to the floor with a punch he gave from only one inch away? That's just two and a half centimeters. He was incredible, that guy. Strong as anything.

"Oh, how's it going?" I asked him. You know, playing the game.

"Oh really well," he said. "Want to see it?"

"Well . . . I . . ."

"Stop the taxi," he said.

"I don't really think . . ."

Now, first rule of a taxi driver is: don't leave your cab. You just don't do it. I mean, anybody could steal it, you know?

"Come on," he said, "over there, there aren't any people."

To this day I really don't know why I did it, but I pulled the taxi to the side of the road. I turned the engine off and put the key in my pocket; you can never be too careful. We both got out. The rain was still pouring down. I looked at him; he was a thin guy, not very big, kind of light. And, well . . . you can see. I'm a big tall guy, well built. I spend time in the gym, like to keep myself fit. Well, you have to, don't you? In fact I used to be on the door at a London nightclub, a bouncer. Yeah, I've done a bit of fighting myself, though not these days. "Well," I thought, "if he tries to steal my taxi, I'll be able to knock him to the ground, flatten him." I wasn't worried, you know.

Then a funny thing happened. He said "Wait!" and he bent down and took his shoes and socks off! Can you imagine that, in the rain? I mean, it was just like tonight, absolutely pouring down. And the funny thing was, I remembered seeing Bruce Lee doing that in his films. He always used to take his shoes and socks off and put them neatly to one side, like he was going to bed or something.

"What are you doing? You crazy?" I asked him.

"Just something I do. Watch this," he said, pointing at a dustbin on the pavement just in front of us.

He stood in his bare feet and put his right fist just in front of the dustbin. Then he punched it.

Well, the next thing I knew the dustbin flew across the street. It was like it had wings, I tell you. Rubbish was flying everywhere! He looked at me, grinning.

"Now just imagine if it was your solar plexus," he said. "Your stomach," he said, like he had to explain to me what a solar plexus was.

I looked at the dustbin lying over the other side of the street. "Well," I thought, "just because he can do that doesn't mean he's Bruce Lee."

"Would you like me to teach you?" he asked.

"Another time maybe," I said. I really wanted to get home to Marlene, and though the punch might be useful in my work, if you know what I mean, I didn't think that now was the moment to learn. Anyway, I was really wet, I mean soaked to the skin.

"It would be my pleasure," he said, still smiling. Then, suddenly, just like that, whoosh! He did a fantastic, really high side-kick at a signpost. It was so fast you could hardly see it. The post fell over and crashed to the ground. Bang!

"Very useful," said 'Bruce', grinning again. "You like it?"

"Oh . . . very nice," I said. "Er . . . shall we get off then?"

I was a bit nervous by this time, you know, looking around to see if anyone had seen what he'd done. Like the police, for example. It'd be just my luck to have them watching us. Luckily there wasn't anybody around. 'Bruce' put his socks and shoes back on and we got back in the cab.

"Why aren't you in Hong Kong, then?" I asked him when we were driving towards Chinatown again. It was a stupid question, I know, but like I say I was kind of nervous. I mean, it's not every day you get a bloke who tells you that he's Bruce Lee in the back of your taxi. And it's not every day he shows you his one-inch punch.

"Well, you know," he said, "I really want to teach my art to the West, so that you can understand my culture." I looked through the mirror at his face. I thought he must be joking, but he looked quite serious.

Now, the thing is, I know a thing or two about fighting. I mean, I grew up in the East End of London and I used to box as a kid. Yeah, I was a boxer. Then later I was a bouncer, like I said. I mean, before I learnt 'the knowledge' and became a taxi driver. The knowledge. Do you know what that is? Well, you have to learn the London streets so that you know them like the back of your hand and it's called the knowledge. Every taxi driver in London has it. It's part of the job – well, it *is* the job. Once you've got the knowledge you're a real London cab driver!

Anyway, on the subject of fighting, I've seen some action and I've seen some pretty good fighters. But this guy, this 'Bruce Lee' was seriously good, far better than the others. I mean, you don't see that kind of speed every day. So I was kind of confused, if you know what I mean. How could he be Bruce Lee? Everybody knew that Bruce Lee was dead. But how could he be that good and *not* be Bruce Lee?

"So, do you think you could teach me?" I asked him. To tell you the truth, it kind of surprised me that I said it; it just came out of my mouth.

"I am sure I could, but are you ready to learn?" he asked.

"I'm not sure what you mean."

"If you were ready to learn, I mean really ready, you wouldn't even feel the rain," said 'Bruce.'

I didn't say anything. I supposed he was right.

"And then there is all that boxing stuff," he said. "It's no use to you. In fact, it gets in the way."

Now, how did he know that I'd been a boxer? Tell me that. I hadn't said anything to him about me being a boxer.

"Like the Zen master said," he went on, "in order to learn you must empty your cup. In other words you must unlearn everything you know so far."

"Well, I really want to try," I said. I mean, it's not every day you meet this kind of person, Bruce Lee or not. He had me kind of interested. "When can we start?"

"Ha!" he said. "You think it is that easy. You are thinking that if this thin little Chinese man can do it, then so can I, because I am big and strong!"

Well, he was right, of course. I *was* thinking that.

"You think that fighting is about aggression," he said. "You don't realise that it's about being strong enough to walk away."

I didn't say anything. He was right though; I supposed I did think that fighting was about being aggressive.

"Are you surprised that I can see what is in your heart?" he asked me.

"Well, I . . ."

"Yes, you must empty your cup," he said again, "and unlearn everything."

"Well," I thought, "easy enough to say, but how do you do that? How do you unlearn everything?"

"Do not try to find me," he went on. "Remember that in Zen they say that when you seek, you will not find. I will find you."

"What do you . . . ?"

"Shh," he said, and put his fingers to his lips.

Well, by now we'd arrived in Chinatown, and he paid me and jumped out of the taxi, quick as a flash. We were outside a restaurant on Gerrard Street. It was one of those typical Chinatown places, with red lights everywhere. I looked out into the rain as he ran towards the restaurant. And then comes the strangest part of this whole story. This is the bit where you're going to think I'm telling you lies. He just disappeared. I mean vanished! First he was there and then he was gone. I saw him outside the restaurant and then, whoof! He disappeared. Difficult to believe eh? But it's true, sure as my name is Ricky Thomas.

Well, I rubbed my eyes a bit. At first I thought he must have gone into the restaurant so I went in to have a look for him. Inside there were a few people having dinner, you know, people who'd been to the theatre or whatever. I looked around the tables. Then I asked the waiters and even the manager. I described him, but no, they hadn't seen him. They didn't know who I was talking about.

So I left the restaurant and drove home. What else could I do? On the way I thought about everything: the punch, the kick, what he said about the cup and my heart, telling me not to look for him and then the way he disappeared like that. It all went through my mind. To tell you the truth, when I really thought about it, I felt that maybe I'd just been working too hard, you know. Perhaps I'd imagined it all. I mean it was all so strange. Except that how could I have imagined it all?

Anyway, I just wanted to go home to see Marlene. I didn't even phone her on the mobile – thought I'd give her a surprise. Come to think of it, that was strange in itself. I never went home without ringing her first.

I got home and stopped the cab outside my third-floor flat in Maxwell Gardens. I looked up at the window and I could see from the light that Marlene was watching television. Probably one of those old Hollywood films that she liked so much, I thought. I suddenly felt really happy that I was going to see her, you know, after all that. I wished that I'd picked up some flowers for her, or some chocolates.

It was still raining hard and I wanted to get in fast, but even so I checked all the doors on the taxi, like I always do. Where I live is full of car thieves and I didn't want them to have a good night. This cab's my pride and joy, you know, and my way of making a living, so it's important to me. I checked the back doors and then I noticed something on the floor of the cab, like a dark shape. I opened the door again and felt the shape. It was the Chinese guy's parcel! The one he was carrying when he got into my cab.

"Well," I thought, "I'm not going to do anything about it tonight. I may as well take it inside and sort it out tomorrow." I took hold of the brown paper parcel and ran inside. I got into the lift and had a look at the package in the light. It was soft, as if it was full of clothes, and there was no name or address on it. I had no idea how I was going to get it back to 'Bruce', especially since he'd disappeared off the face of the earth. Still, I don't mind telling you that I felt somehow happy that I had it. It meant that there was at least a chance that he might try and contact me to get his parcel back.

I went upstairs. "Ricky!" Marlene shouted as soon as I put the key in the front door. But she didn't sound very happy; it was like she was upset that I was home early. I walked down the hall and opened the door of the living room. Then I got the shock of my life, I tell you. I went in and she was there, in my living room, with another man! He was a thin, blond-haired guy. As soon as he saw me he jumped up from the sofa and tried to get out of the door. Marlene jumped up too. "Ricky, you're early," she said, "and you didn't phone . . ."

"Well, I can see that you weren't expecting me," I said. I was mad, I can tell you. The man was standing in front of me and I really felt like punching him. He was a thin little man, not much meat on him, if you know what I mean, and I could have really hurt him. Tell you the truth, I felt like killing him! And that's what the old me would have done, believe me. But something strange happened that night. Suddenly, I felt calm all over. I didn't feel like punching him any more. I heard the Chinese guy's voice in my head. "You think that fighting is about aggression. You don't realise that it's about being strong enough to walk away." Suddenly I could see everything. I could see that this wasn't the first time. I could see that Marlene wasn't faithful to me and that she never had been. I could see that she didn't love me. It came to me, you know. It just suddenly hit me. It was like, what do they call it? A *revelation*, mate, that's it.

So that was the first thing that changed. Once I knew that Marlene didn't love me, I didn't want her any more. It was living a lie and I knew immediately that I couldn't do that. So, next day she left, and I haven't seen her since. "I'm looking for the right one," I said to myself, "and I'm not interested in second best."

So, anyway, with all the upset, I totally forgot about the parcel I'd found in the back of the cab. But the next day, once Marlene had gone, I remembered. I didn't know what to do with it and I was really curious about what was inside. I tore open the brown paper wrapping and found . . . a pair of blue pyjamas, made of silk. I held them up to have a good look. I just stood there, staring. The top was a Chinese-style jacket with a stand-up collar. The bottoms were just silk trousers. They were both deep, midnight blue, and really lovely. They looked incredible in my living room. It sounds funny, but it was like there was suddenly a lot of light, if you know what I mean. Like a ray of sunshine. I knew that I had to keep them.

Then, I know it sounds funny, mate, but it was like that ray of sunshine started to have an effect on me, on my life. I don't know what it was, but something began that night. Getting rid of Marlene was just the start of it all. It was like the truth started to come out. Things started to change in me. A few days later I thought, "What am I doing with my life? Do I just want to be a taxi driver forever?" I mean, it's all right, but there's more to life than driving a cab. There's more knowledge than knowledge of the streets of London, if you know what I mean. I started to think about college, you know. I left school when I was sixteen, but there's no reason I can't go back. So now I go to college one day a week, getting some qualifications you know, trying to improve myself. And then I'll stop being a cab driver. I want to start my own business. I mean, you've only got one life, haven't you, mate?

And I know this sounds weird, but I'm sure it all has something to do with those pyjamas. I mean that's when it all started. I couldn't help wondering about them. I mean, they looked kind of familiar to me. I was sure I'd seen them before. So about a week after I'd come home with the parcel, I got myself a beer and got out all my old Bruce Lee videos. *The Chinese Connection, Enter the Dragon . . . Return of the Dragon*, all of them. I sat there watching them for hours. Finally I found what I was looking for. *Return of the Dragon*, it was. There he was, Bruce Lee, wearing blue pyjamas, just like the ones in my wardrobe!

I got down on the floor next to the television screen to take a closer look at the blue silk pyjamas. I put the video on pause and stared at them. Yeah, there was no doubt about it; they were 'my' blue pyjamas. Well, they weren't really pyjamas, you know. It was a suit, his kung fu suit. But they looked exactly like the blue pyjamas in my bedroom. They *were* the blue pyjamas in my bedroom!

Yeah, things started changing in me, no doubt about it. Over the months there were lots of things. I'm training to run my own business, like I said. I stopped smoking and drinking too much, you know. I started going to the gym again, went jogging and lost a bit of weight. Just looking after my body. Different things started to become important, you know. Somehow I started to respect myself.

So that's it really. It's a mystery to me, a complete mystery, mate. It's a year ago now and I still think about it every day. But the thing is, I take care of those blue pyjamas, I mean they're hanging up in the wardrobe, nice and tidy and clean. So that if this guy, this 'Bruce Lee' came back for them they'd be just the same as they were when he left them. I know it's kind of stupid, but he'd know that I'd looked after them.

And I think about what he said about not looking for him, about him finding me. And funny thing is, I feel like I'm kind of waiting. Waiting and getting ready. Yeah, it's a funny old world. There you are, mate. Chinatown. That'll be ten pounds.'

'I'm here Ricky,' said a voice from the back of the cab. The taxi driver turned around and looked into the blackness in the back of the cab. But he couldn't see anyone. 'I think you've started,' said the voice. It was 'Bruce Lee's' voice, he was sure. The cab driver rubbed his eyes, but still there was no one there. 'You're on the way to the knowledge.'

Fifteen Hundred Words

'Remember,' her teacher, Kit, said. 'Remember what you saw tonight from a true Japanese master. Self-control. Holding back emotion. Now, homework. Write a story that shows the relationship between two people. Fifteen hundred words. Be delicate. No drama. And you,' she said, looking at Abi, and smiling, 'no dead bodies, please.'

Abi left the Vancouver Film School and walked quickly past the guys begging for change on Hastings Street. Her whole body felt light with excitement. She smiled when she thought about Kit's words. Yes, Abi thought, she could write thrillers. Dead bodies were no problem; now it was time to develop some new skills.

She turned onto Dunsmuir Street and went towards the skytrain station, thinking about the film they'd watched in her screenwriting class that evening. It was *Tokyo Story* by the Japanese director, Ozu, made in 1953. It had always been one of Abi's favourite films, and it was wonderful to see it again. The acting was outstanding, she thought, feelings were indicated powerfully by just a look or a turn of the head, a handkerchief held in a hand. It was all very Japanese. As you watched it you felt that it had a kind of universal truth. Yes, very Japanese. She had studied Japanese back in London and a word came to her from the depths of her memory. *Enryo*. It meant calmness and self-control, or holding back. Yes, *Tokyo Story* showed *Enryo* all right. Nothing much seemed to happen, but by the end of the film you felt you really knew the characters and cared deeply about them. Such a change from typical Hollywood films, thought Abi, as she ran up the steps to the skytrain station at Stadium.

Abi stood and waited for the skytrain to Broadway. A bitter December wind blew down off the coastal mountains and through Stadium station. She shivered and closed her warm winter jacket around her. She looked at her watch; it was nine thirty-five. Ray would be on the skytrain and they would go home together to their apartment on Commercial Drive. They had decided not to use their four-wheel drive car in the city; it was hard to park and the public transport system was good. Just two stops on the skytrain and then the number twenty bus to their apartment. They always met up on the skytrain on Wednesday evenings and went home together. Abi went to her class and Ray stayed at work late. He was a commercial lawyer and his office was downtown.

Abi looked at the mountains that surrounded the city. The snow sparkled in the moonlight and here and there she could see the lights of the ski runs. Sometimes she just couldn't believe her luck, living in Vancouver. It was simply beautiful. It had these fantastic mountains and an incredible coastline. At weekends, when Ray didn't have work to do, they could go skiing at Grouse Mountain or Whistler. But it wasn't just skiing and the outdoor lifestyle. It was also that Vancouver had so many opportunities for writers. They called it Hollywood North; the city was full of directors, producers, actors and writers. Abi had known for some time that it was the right place to work on her screenwriting career, so when Ray's firm had wanted to transfer him to Vancouver six months ago, it had been a great opportunity.

The clean white skytrain arrived at the station. Abi got on and looked around for Ray. She found him right at the end of the train. He looked so English in his dark suit, so out of place somehow. He smiled thinly at her. He looked grey and tired. Now she thought about it, he always looked tired these days. Well, it was true that he had to work long hours at the office. She kissed him lightly on the cheek. 'Good day?'

'Oh, it was all right, I suppose,' he said, staring blankly ahead. 'Just too much work. The boss has just signed another contract. And I've got to go to Toronto next week.' Ray's boss was always sending Ray to Toronto or Montreal on business.

'Oh really?' said Abi. 'Toronto . . .' The excitement of her film class still burned inside her.

There was a silence for a few moments.

'Main Street, Science World,' came the automated voice. The train slowed down as it approached the station.

'We saw a fantastic film tonight,' said Abi, as the train moved out of the station.

'Oh yeah? God, I'm hungry.'

'Japanese. *Tokyo Story.*'

'Didn't have time for lunch today.'

'It's really exciting,' said Abi. 'I mean, what you can do with film.'

'Starving.'

'I mean, I know that Shakespeare said action is eloquence; that it speaks for itself, and it's true because action is important, but it doesn't have to be extreme action. I mean, if you think about it . . .'

'Broadway, Commercial Drive' said the automated voice.

Abi and Ray stood up automatically. They walked along the platform and down the steps to the bus stop.

'I hate this bus. It's always late,' Ray said as they waited for bus twenty in the cold. He always complained about the bus. The corner of Commercial and Broadway, where they had to wait for it, was one of the coldest, windiest places in the city. Then the bus itself was always full of, well, interesting people. Someone was always shouting out, starting an argument or talking nonsense to you. This was the darker side of Vancouver. It wasn't that it was a bad city. It was just that Vancouver was full of people who were a little 'different'. Especially on public transport. Abi loved it. As a writer, she found the bus endlessly exciting. It was full of stories and completely unpredictable. But Ray couldn't see its charm, and never stopped complaining about it.

After a cold ten-minute wait, the bus arrived and they found a seat well inside.

'Got a toonie for a cup of coffee, miss?'

The bearded man in the seat in front had turned round and was looking at Abi. 'Toonie' was the Canadian word for a two-dollar piece. She looked at the man carefully. He looked sick. He was thin and grey, and his clothes and beard were dirty. She had seen the bus driver let him on the bus for free. The kindest drivers sometimes did that.

Abi started to reach into her pocket for a two-dollar piece.

'Forget it,' said Ray to the man.

'But the lady . . .'

'Forget the lady,' said Ray firmly. 'Abi, don't.'

Abi looked at Ray. His cheeks were suddenly red.

The man with the beard leaned towards Abi. His breath smelt bad.

'Listen,' said Ray, losing his temper. 'Leave us alone.'

The man ignored him and just carried on moving his face towards Abi.

'Let me give him something,' said Abi softly, trying to calm the situation down.

But Ray was not to be calmed. He jumped out of his seat.

'Ray, don't . . .'

But Ray had now gone beyond words. He picked the man up by his dirty collar and pushed him to the floor of the bus. The man landed heavily.

'Leave us alone!' Ray shouted again.

By now the whole bus was shouting. Some of the passengers were moving towards the man on the floor. One man asked the driver to stop the bus. A woman helped the bearded man to his feet.

'Come on,' said Ray. 'Let's get off this awful bus!'

'No, let's . . .'

'Get off the bus!' Ray's face was white with anger.

'No,' said Abi. 'Let's just go home.'

Ray looked at her and shook his head. 'Let me get off!' he shouted to the driver, who immediately opened the doors.

The bus moved off, leaving Ray walking down Commercial Drive, past the fast food places and shops, staring hard at the pavement.

On the bus, the passengers calmed down quickly. It had been a fairly normal scene for bus twenty. The bearded man sat down again.

As the bus approached her stop, Abi got up. She took a toonie out of her pocket and gave it to the bearded man.

'Why, thank you, miss,' he said, smiling through his broken teeth. 'That's really kind of you.'

Abi nodded and stood waiting for the automatic doors to open.

'Take my advice, darlin',' continued the man. 'Leave him. He just ain't your type. Ain't your type at all . . .'

Abi turned and looked at the man. She stepped from the bus onto the sidewalk, and her face broke into a smile.

As she walked the two hundred meters to the apartment, Abi thought about Ray and reflected that the end is not always a big event. It can be slow and insistent, like waves on a rock. Until one day the rock is no longer there.

Well, she thought, at least Kit would be pleased. Not too much drama. Certainly no dead bodies. Just fifteen hundred words. Exactly.

North Sea Eyes

Love is a dangerous emotion, let me tell you. And it always happens when you're least expecting it. It creeps up on you and jumps on you out of the blue. It grabs you by the throat, shakes you and says, 'I'm here! You'd better take notice of me!'

I mean, think about it. One minute you're going along very nicely, thank you. You get up every morning for work and you come home every evening. You make dinner. You watch your favourite TV program on Tuesdays and Thursdays. You go out, you come in. You have a drink on Friday nights. The highlight of your week is lunch out on Sundays. That's life as you know it. At least you think you're alive, but then *real* life comes along and does a little dance in front of you and you realize that you've been half dead.

That's the way it was when I met Ria.

One minute I was just going along like this, bored but kind of OK. Well at least I was healthy. Next thing I knew I was out late at night, freezing to death, doing all kinds of strange things. And it seemed to me that I just had to do them; somehow I didn't have any choice.

Now I don't know about you, but there's a certain pattern to my falling in love. First of all, it always happens in winter, so it's freezing cold. October, November and December are the usual months, and they're cold in Holland, really cold. And in The Hague the wind comes off the sea and goes right through you like a knife. Not the kind of weather for hanging around on street corners or in telephone boxes, but that's always what I end up doing. One day I'm going to bed at nine thirty with a good book, the next I'm out at one o'clock in the morning, knowing that I'm going to be exhausted the next day. Exhausted, but excited. Then comes a cold, or even worse, flu. I'd like to fall in love in summer, but it never happens that way.

Then there's the poetry. Suddenly I start writing poetry; it just pours out of me. And it's all deep meaningful stuff that has to be written in the early hours of the morning, usually accompanied by lots of alcohol. So the next day, on top of the cold I already have, I have a hangover from the drink. It's a miracle that my boss hasn't sacked me.

And the worst bit is when I realise that there's probably another man in her life. And of course he's really good-looking and has a sports car and a big bank account.

So everything followed more or less the usual pattern with Ria. First came the cold and the poems. I hadn't seen the good-looking boyfriend yet, but I had the feeling that it was just a matter of time. There *was* something about Ria that was different, though. She was different from other girls. First of all there was her job. She was a tram driver.

But let me tell you a little bit about myself, because no doubt you're wondering what an English guy is doing living in Holland, in The Hague to be exact. Well, my name's Harry Brent, I'm twenty-nine and I've been here for two years. I work for an international import and export company, JGD. They're based in Manchester but have offices all over Europe. They sent me here to work in their Dutch office. I'll probably be here for another two or three years. Import and export. Sounds kind of boring, eh? Well, it's OK really, and Holland is an interesting country. For one thing, you can more or less do what you want here. I mean, it's very liberal, very tolerant. And although I don't really do much that's exciting, if you know what I mean, I like it. I like the atmosphere and just the thought that if I wanted to take all my clothes off in the middle of the street, no one would care. No. No one would even notice.

So, like I say, I live in The Hague. It's not as beautiful or as exciting as Amsterdam, but it has its advantages. The best thing about it is that it's near a place called Scheveningen, which is almost unpronounceable but lovely. It has long soft sandy beaches, which are wonderful for walks. And the sea here, the North Sea, is just beautiful, a soft blue-grey.

I go to the beach a lot. The traffic in The Hague is pretty bad, but it has good public transport. The noisy red trams and their rails are a familiar sight and that's how I get about. Number one to work, number three to the city centre. And number eleven from my place down to the beach. I live alone in one of those typical tall Dutch houses on a little street between the city centre and the beach. I often go down to the beach after work and at weekends, to walk and relax and look at the sea. Which brings me back to Ria.

I first noticed Ria when I was going to the beach on tram eleven one Sunday afternoon. It was early October and a beautiful cold bright day. The tram suddenly stopped somewhere in the middle of nowhere; something was stuck on the rails. It happens a lot, and I didn't take much notice until I looked out of the window and saw the tram driver removing a small piece of wood. Now, you can get on a tram in Holland without seeing the driver, and that's exactly what I'd done. But now I saw her, I couldn't take my eyes off her. I've never seen a tram driver wear a uniform as well as Ria did. She was tall and slim. And even from a distance I could see that she was beautiful, with long dark hair. Really attractive. She was wearing a skirt, unlike most female tram drivers who usually wear trousers. And she had legs that seemed to go on forever. Yeah, she was different.

But the most amazing thing about Ria was her eyes, which I noticed straight away, and which were the exact colour of the North Sea, a lovely soft blue-grey. And those eyes kind of grabbed me, that's the only way I can put it, so that I couldn't think of anything else. I'd been grabbed by the throat.

Well, she got back into the tram and we carried on towards the beach. I moved up the tram so that I could be nearer to her. And I just looked at her all the way to the beach, though I tried not to let her see. I was kind of dazed, as if I'd been hit on the head. I was confused, I don't mind telling you.

Anyway, the number eleven stops at the beach, on the south side of Scheveningen not too far from the port; it's the end of the tramline. It waits for ten or fifteen minutes, turns round and goes back to the city. I got out and just sort of hung around for a while, looking at Ria but pretending I wasn't looking. The idea of going away was scary; I might never see her again. After a few minutes, Ria got out of the tram and talked for a while to another tram driver. That's when I discovered that she was called Ria, because I heard him shout something to her. It looked like she was going to drive tram eleven back to the city.

I had a little time so I went over to the other side of the road and bought some chips from a little shop near the beach, keeping my eyes on the tram, and Ria, all the time. Then I walked back slowly to the tram, eating my chips and mayonnaise – I know it's a strange combination, but I've got used to it. I got back on the tram and went back to the city with Ria.

So that was it really. For the next two weeks I spent all of my spare time on trams, especially on tram eleven, hoping that she would be the driver, and that I'd get to see her. I got to love that little red tram; it was kind of comforting. I also spent a lot of time waiting for trams, which is when I got the cold. I got to know her routine, and I managed to see a lot of her one way or another. And at nights I would go home to my house and write poetry.

Anyway, one late afternoon I was waiting for the tram on the platform. It pulled up and, as luck would have it, Ria was driving. I was feeling kind of brave that particular day, and I got on at the front, just so I could really see her. As I got on, she smiled at me and said, '*goede middag*,' which means, 'Good afternoon.' Well, not so unusual you might think, but I knew when she said it that she recognised me. It was the way her eyes met mine. I don't remember much about that tram ride, I can tell you! I could feel my face burning red. I was completely overcome with it all. I kept reliving that moment when she had said '*goede middag*' for days afterwards.

Well, from then on we said hello to each other quite often. I was working towards asking her out, you know, kind of trying to find the courage. Finally, one Friday evening, I knew I had to go for it. For one thing, it was starting to look very strange, you know, me following her around like that. I didn't want anyone to think I was some kind of weird guy who follows women – you know, a stalker or something.

So this particular Friday evening I left work at six o'clock as usual. What I needed was a drink, I thought. Otherwise there was no way I could talk to Ria, not *really* talk, I mean.

The office where I work is near the centre of the city, on a street called Korte Voorhout, so I decided to go to the Dudok. It's a big new bar just a few minutes' walk away. A cool kind of place, if you know what I mean. A fashionable place to be seen. I sometimes went there for a quick drink after work, just because it's near the office.

The Dudok was already crowded; it was a popular spot for an early evening drink, what the Dutch call a *borrel*. Yeah, it was definitely *borrel* time. I found a place at the bar and drank a couple of beers quickly. There was a new barman there, a friendly sort of bloke who came over and started chatting. 'English, eh?' he asked. Turned out his brother had gone to work in London. I didn't have the heart to tell him I'd never been there. I mean, just Heathrow airport. So I just nodded when he mentioned Notting Hill and Chiswick.

'Lovely part of London, Chiswick,' he said.

'Gorgeous,' I said.

'Another beer?'

'Er, I'd better not,' I said weakly.

'Come on,' he said. 'It's . . . how do you say it . . .? On the house.'

Anyway, he was a friendly guy, like I said. He kept coming over to talk to me from time to time, and I kept drinking. I was thinking about what I was going to say to Ria, to be honest, and I wasn't getting very far. After about an hour, he asked me, 'So, what are you doing all alone on a Friday evening, Harry?' By then we were on first-name terms. His was Hans.

Well, I'd had a few beers by then, so I told him about Ria. I told him about tram eleven and the fact that I'd decided to try to get to know her and to ask her out.

Hans smiled at me with big round eyes. 'Oh, well, good luck, Harry,' he said. 'And I hope she doesn't disappoint you. They say that Dutch women are really strong! You take care of yourself.'

Funny thing to say, I thought. Anyway, I had a few more beers, and before I knew it was eleven o'clock! I felt like I knew London like the back of my hand, but that wasn't the point. The point was to talk to Ria and ask her out, I told myself. It was time to get on tram eleven. I wasn't *totally* drunk, though I must say I'd had enough. I said goodbye to the barman and ran off to catch tram one so that I could get on tram eleven at the Hollands Spoor Station.

On the platform I stood where the front of the tram would stop to make sure that it was Ria driving. The first driver was a man, some big blond guy with a moustache, so I waited for the next. Ah, there she was! She looked as attractive as ever, with those lovely North Sea eyes. I got on at the back of the tram this time. I didn't want her to see me before I was ready, if you know what I mean. I put my tram ticket in the little machine and sat right at the back. It was late October by now and it was really cold and windy.

As a matter of fact, it's always windy in The Hague. But the moon was up and it was nice and clear.

I still wasn't sure how I was going to approach her but, like I said, I had to try. Well, I sat there and sat there and I couldn't think of a way to talk to her – I mean, say more than 'Good evening.' What do you say? 'Do you come here often?' I just couldn't imagine myself asking her, if you know what I mean. Truth is, I'm not very good with women, I suppose.

So, before I knew it, we were at the beach and everybody had to get off. There were about ten people on the tram, mostly people who lived up there, I reckoned, and they all got off and walked away pretty quickly. I got off quickly too so that Ria wouldn't see me. I went and stood behind the tram shelter, where I could see her but she couldn't see me. It was obvious from the way that she collected her stuff together that she was going off duty. I tried to think of a way of hanging around for a while and kept my eye on her.

Then, she said something to another tram driver who was going to take the tram back to the city centre and then she set off walking quickly in the direction of the port. I didn't know what to do, to be honest, seeing her go like that, so I followed her. Oh, I know it looked like I was stalking her, which is exactly what I said I didn't want to do. But it seemed like my only choice. Like I said, love is a dangerous emotion.

Well, by now the wind was blowing up a storm over the North Sea and the sky was full of huge black clouds. Dutch weather is like that old joke: 'If you don't like it, just wait a while and it'll change.' The sky reminded me of one of those paintings you see at the Rijksmuseum in Amsterdam, painted by Rembrandt or Vermeer or someone. It wasn't raining yet, but it was only a matter of time.

I kept quite far behind Ria. Well, I didn't have much choice, to be honest. She was a very fast walker! She kept up a quick pace along the seafront, trying to get home before the storm blew up, I suppose. I was almost running, just to keep her in sight! I suppose I was drunk too, to be honest, and it's hard to move fast when you've drunk too much. There were a few people still around, coming out of the bars and restaurants in Scheveningen and walking to their cars, or just taking the sea air. I didn't look too strange. It was about midnight by now. I was thinking to myself 'this is stupid,' and telling myself that I was a coward but, like I say, I couldn't help it.

The beach front at Scheveningen is long, and there's a kind of wide path that goes right down towards the port. That was obviously where Ria was heading, so I was thinking that she had to live somewhere near the port. Part of the old fishing village, the original Scheveningen, is down there. So I carried on walking, following her.

The weather at the beach changes pretty quickly, like I said, and, sure enough, before long it started raining quite hard, that kind of horizontal rain you get around here. I didn't have an umbrella of course, so soon I was completely soaked. After about twenty minutes' walk, we got near the port. At the beginning of the port area, there are a lot of fish restaurants and small bars. But by now they were almost all closed, and the place was nearly deserted. Ria looked round at one point, but I was far enough away that she couldn't recognize me.

Then we got into the port itself. There were quite a few boats there: a few local fishing boats, and some ships with the names of English ports on them. Around the harbour itself it was pretty dark, and the only noise I could hear was the sound of Ria's heels on the pavement.

Right in the corner of the harbour there's a little bar called De Hoek. It's a place where the fishermen go, and some Scheveningen locals. I'd never been in there myself, though I'd heard people at the office talk about it. It had a reputation as a wild kind of place. It was still open; I could see a kind of dim yellow light and there was music and voices coming from inside. I looked at my watch. It was one o'clock! It was late, but the bar was so far away from any houses that it could probably stay open as long as it liked, I thought.

Anyway, Ria walked over towards it, opened the door and went right in. Odd, I thought. Did she live there, or was she just going in for a quick drink before bed? Hard to say. By now the rain had died down a bit, so I decided to wait a little longer. Well, I was already wet through so it didn't matter. Yeah, I know it sounds crazy, but that's what I told you. You do strange things when you're in love.

So I waited quite a while. My mind was working overtime, I can tell you. Did she live here, or did her boyfriend live here? There *had* to be a boyfriend. Perhaps he was a fisherman or sailor! A good-looking sailor with a sports car and a big bank account of course. That would be just my luck.

So there I was, waiting. And I thought, 'Hey, I haven't got anything to lose.' You know what I mean? So what if she's got a boyfriend? It can't be any worse than standing out here, dripping wet and shivering. By now I was like a dog that had just come out of the sea. And it looked like it was going to start raining again. So I walked over to the bar and opened the old wooden door.

The only things I noticed at first were the overpowering smell of cigars, and a fair amount of smoke. I could hear music playing too, sounded like jazz. I looked around, trying to see Ria.

'Are you sure you want to come in here?' I looked up into the face of a huge Dutch guy. He was standing right next to me blowing smoke in my face.

'Er, I'm not sure,' I answered.

'Well, decide,' he said.

The bar was full of people, men mainly, though there were a couple of women too. I looked around for Ria, but I couldn't see her anywhere. I moved away from the tall Dutchman and pushed through the crowd towards the bar. As I moved through the smoke I could see a kind of stage on the other side of the room. And on the stage someone was dancing to the music. After a minute or so, my eyes got used to the smoke and the dim light, and I could see the dancer. It took me a little while to work out that she was completely naked!

Well, I didn't know where to look, I can tell you. The big Dutch guy was looking at me, smiling and watching for my reactions. I sort of smiled back. To be honest, I wanted to leave. I felt kind of embarrassed. But I didn't want to seem foolish or anything, so I acted like it was the most natural thing in the world. I ordered a beer, though it was the last thing I wanted, to tell you the truth. I just wanted to run out of there, Ria or no Ria.

Then the music stopped and everyone clapped. 'Oh good,' I thought, 'this is my chance to get out of here.' But the music started again almost immediately and someone else came onto the stage.

'Look at this,' said the big Dutch guy, pushing my elbow. 'You'll like this!'

I smiled kind of awkwardly, and looked over to the little stage and at the face of the new dancer.

She was wearing a bit more make-up than usual, but there was no mistaking those eyes. It was Ria!

Well, I was shocked, I can tell you! But it got worse. The music started and Ria started taking her clothes off. Everyone in the bar was shouting and whistling. Part of me wanted to leave, but the other part just made me stay there. I couldn't move. Little by little, Ria's clothes came off until she was completely naked. And then came the greatest shock of all, because then I saw that there *was* something about Ria that was different. She *was* different from other girls. And it wasn't only that she was a tram driver. She was a man!

'Aaagh!' I sort of screamed and moved quickly towards the door.

'See what I mean?' said the big Dutch guy behind me, laughing.

I ran outside. The Dutch guy followed me, shouting, 'So, you like our entertainment, do you, little English boy?'

A bit rude, I thought, calling me 'little', but I thought I'd let it pass. I ran as fast as I could.

I ran all the way back home. I couldn't help thinking about what Hans had said about 'strong women'. He didn't know how right he was.

*   *   *

Yeah, there are times when life comes and grabs you by the throat.

So, all that happened about six months ago. Since then, things have, well, calmed down a bit. I get up every morning for work and I come home every evening. I make dinner. I watch my favourite TV program on Tuesdays and Thursdays. I go out, I come in. I have a drink on a Friday night. The highlight of my week is lunch out on Sundays. OK, it's boring, but to tell the truth I kind of like it. I'm happy.

But I'm really not looking forward to the winter.

End Point

Austin murders

AUSTIN, TEXAS
Three people were shot dead and several more injured in an incident in a motel in Austin yesterday. So far the Austin police have not released the names of the victims, or the suspect.

As Paul Boyle got on the plane in Chicago, he remembered how he had wanted to go to Austin ever since he was a teenager. It was the music, really, that attracted him. And now he had his chance. United's two-week tour to the States, to get the Americans more interested in football – or soccer, as they called it – was finished. There was just enough time to fly down there before the start of the new season back in England. He would spend a couple of days in Austin and have a look around. It would be fun to stay in a motel, instead of a five-star hotel, and see some good bands. Just have fun.

'Why don't you and the kids come with me?' Paul had said to his wife Karen. But she had been concerned to get the children settled down back home in Manchester again. It was little Darren's first year at school, and she wanted him to have the best possible start. And their second child Courtney was still only eleven months old. It was hard travelling with two small children.

'No, darling,' she had said. 'You go off for a few days on

your own, enjoy yourself, and I'll get back home.' The truth was that she wasn't too keen on the States. Two weeks of it was quite enough. She was looking forward to getting back into her routine again.

As Paul Boyle sat down in his business class seat, he thought how nice it was to get a little time to himself. It was a busy life being a star footballer. All in all, it was rare that he was on his own these days. There was his club, United, and then the national team too. That meant a lot of training every week, and then there were the advertisers who paid so much to use his name. It was all very hard work.

Not that he was complaining. 'I'm the luckiest guy in the world,' he always said when he was interviewed. 'After all, I get paid a lot of money for doing what I love.' Not only was he 'the most talented footballer of his generation', as a leading sports journalist had described him, but he was also handsome and intelligent. And he had a wonderful family. He had everything going for him.

And now there was talk that he would be made captain of the England team for the preparations for the European Cup. He hadn't even talked to Karen about that yet. After all, it wasn't official, and he wanted it so much that he was scared of mentioning it. He didn't want her to be disappointed if it didn't happen.

He smiled to himself when he thought about it, though. It was what he had always dreamed of! As a kid he had sat and watched players like Bryan Robson and Gary Lineker lead England. At night he had slept in his little bedroom with pictures of great England players, like Bobby Moore and Geoff Hurst, on his walls. They were like gods to him. Now he was one of them. Sometimes he had to pinch himself to make sure he wasn't dreaming! To wear the three lions on your shirt at all was an incredible honour, but to be captain of England! It would be the peak of his career. No footballer could wish for more.

'Thanks,' he said, smiling widely, as the flight attendant gave him his fresh orange juice.

*   *   *

'Yesterday morning, at about ten o'clock, forty-four-year-old Grace Kent left her home in Galveston, Texas and went for a walk by the ocean. This was her usual routine on Sunday mornings, generally returning home by twelve noon. But yesterday she still hadn't returned home by one o'clock. At about one thirty, her husband, Bob Kent, forty-six, rang the Coast Guard and a search began. The Coast Guard found her clothes on the beach at seven o'clock in the evening. It is now feared that she drowned in the storm that hit the Gulf coast yesterday afternoon. Jim Lean, chief of the Galveston Coast Guard Station, said in a statement yesterday "If Mrs Kent was in the water when the storm came on shore in the Gulf of Mexico, it's very unlikely that she could have survived."'

Grace Kent sat in a coffee shop and stared hard at the television screen. She watched the pictures and listened to the presenter almost as if it were about someone else. 'Galveston woman may have drowned' said the headline at the bottom of the screen. So, thought Grace, she had managed to disappear. And now, it seemed, she had drowned as well!

She looked at the photo of herself on the screen. They'd chosen the one of her on vacation in Palm Springs about eight years ago, the one that had always stood over the fireplace in the living room. She looked almost happy and relaxed there. She had long blonde hair that she wore loose. The woman now sitting on the bench looked very different. Her hair was jet black and tied back, and she wore thick unattractive glasses, like the ones worn by librarians in films. Yes, she thought, she had disguised herself well. Nobody could have known that the woman in the grey jacket and the glasses was Grace Kent.

Grace paid for her coffee and went outside. The air was warm and she could feel a threatening wind from the Gulf of Mexico. Another storm on the way, no doubt. Perhaps even a hurricane. She went past the shops lining the sidewalk, past the Texas State Bank where she'd worked for nine years. Then she walked hurriedly across the road and into the Greyhound bus station on 25th Street.

'A ticket to Austin,' she said to the man in the ticket office.

Grace picked up a small black overnight bag from the baggage room at the bus station and got on the bus to Austin. She chose a window seat near the back of the bus and placed the bag above her head. She took off her jacket and sat down. Within minutes the bus was crawling slowly out of the station. It was about two hundred miles to Austin and the journey would take well over five hours. Grace sat back, thankful that the bus was not full and she could sit alone.

As the bus left Galveston and joined the freeway, Grace was aware that she felt lighter. As long as she could remember, she had loved travelling – being on the move. Grace couldn't help smiling to herself. Now she was not only on the move but dead as well. There was freedom in that. Oh, eventually she would tell everyone that she was still alive. Bob and the kids. But for now she would enjoy her moment of complete and absolute freedom.

*   *   *

Colonel Tim Parker of the British Army looked at himself in the full-length mirror that stood in the hallway of his house. He liked what he saw. His suit was neat and well pressed. His shoes shone. He smoothed back his hair and put on his hat, adjusting it to exactly the angle he liked best. Yes, at fifty-five he was still a fine figure of a man, tall and athletic. He was ready for one of the final journeys of his tour of duty in Central America, almost the final journey of his career. In three weeks he would be leaving for England and in just a few months he would be retiring from the army.

In the meantime, the colonel had been invited to Austin, Texas, to represent the British Army at an international conference on security. Today he would fly from Guatemala City airport to Dallas, then through to Austin.

''Bye, dear,' he called to his wife.

Victoria Parker came out of the kitchen and kissed her husband goodbye. She was a slim pretty woman in her early fifties. Though she was greying now, it was not hard to see why she had caught the eye of the young Major Parker at an army dance thirty years earlier.

''Bye darling,' she said. 'See you on Sunday. And don't forget to take some time off to see the bats!'

The colonel smiled. He was crazy about bats. He'd always been amazed at these small mouse-like animals with big ears which only flew at night. In fact, bats were his main hobby. One of the attractions of going to Austin was that it was the city with the largest population of bats in the world. They moved up from Mexico in spring to give birth. And the best time to see them was right now in August, when the young joined their parents in nightly flights from under the Congress Avenue Bridge. Apparently, there were so many bats that it could take forty-five minutes for them all to leave the bridge. Some estimates said that there were one and a half million bats. The colonel was really looking forward to seeing the sight. He felt like an excited schoolboy.

The colonel opened the fine old wooden door of the house and stepped out. His driver had brought the Land Rover from the garage round to the wide driveway. The colonel got into the car as he had done so many times before and put his two-way radio on the little shelf in front of him. The automatic gates of the house opened and they drove out, taking the third of the five alternative routes to the airport.

*   *   *

Joe Stefano didn't much like working at the hotel, but he figured it was a job. And in San Antonio, Texas, jobs were hard to come by. He'd got the job because of his wife Rita, in fact because of Rita's father Jack. Joe couldn't stand old Jack Vazquez; he was an interfering old guy who thought his darling daughter Rita was far too good for Joe. Joe hated having to be obliged to him, even grateful to him, but he didn't have much choice.

Anyway, Jack had a friend called Henriquez who owned

a hotel in downtown San Antonio, and he found a job in the hotel kitchen for Joe at Jack's request.

'You'll have to start at the bottom,' said old Henriquez, 'just like everybody else. I don't want people accusing me of promoting the relatives of my friends!'

Great! What was the point of having 'friends' if they couldn't find you a nice easy job? Joe tried to stick at it. He spent his days washing dirty dishes, peeling potatoes and cleaning floors.

Joe was an anxious, nervous man of about thirty-five, with curly black hair and deep blue eyes. He was handsome enough, and he had that charm that women sometimes fall for. Rita had certainly fallen for it.

'Don't worry about starting at the bottom, darling,' Rita kept saying. 'It's only a matter of time. Little by little, they'll see that you're a good hard-working man and they'll move you up.'

Joe wondered whether that was true. In his worst moments, he imagined that he would end up a worn-out old man, washing dirty plates. And the truth was that he had a terrible temper, which meant that he didn't like taking orders from anyone. Most days he had to make a big effort not to hit the kitchen manager, a thin, ugly guy. Sooner or later, something had to go wrong; it always did.

It lasted three months.

The day it ended was a normal Friday at the hotel. There was a big group of businessmen in for a fancy lunch, so the restaurant was busy. But it was always busy. One of the cooks asked Joe to bring him a large pan of water. Joe dropped the water on the floor. The kitchen manager ran over and shouted at him, calling him a stupid idiot, and told him to clean it up immediately. Joe saw red. He lifted up his fist. He felt like hitting the manager, but took it out on his kitchen instead. He went crazy. He threw all the pans onto the floor, and within seconds the kitchen was swimming in boiling water and broccoli. He ruined all the food and burned one of the cooks so badly that he had to be taken to hospital.

Joe was sacked immediately.

'Get out!' shouted the kitchen manager. 'And never let me see you in my kitchen again!'

Joe wondered how he was going to tell Rita.

*   *   *

'Footballer, eh?' said the large Texan man sitting next to Paul Boyle on his flight from Dallas to Austin. 'You must make a lot of money, then.'

Boyle smiled and nodded. He didn't mind this kind of exchange; in fact it was one of the things he liked about the States. But it was exactly the kind of thing that drove Karen mad. Strangers would start conversations with you, and ask you the most personal questions.

'Well, yes,' he answered smiling, 'I suppose so.'

Paul had often thought that if he hadn't been a footballer, he would have been a musician. He'd always played the guitar, even as a kid, and he still played sometimes with his mates back home in Manchester. When he had time, that is. His passion was the blues, which was why Austin was so attractive. He loved Blind Lemon Jefferson and Blind Willie Johnson and all those guys. Why were they always blind, he wondered. His plan was to go to Antone's Blues Club while he was in Austin and listen to some really good live music.

In fact, he thought, as the plane started its approach into Austin-Bergstrom Airport, there might even be time to go tonight. It was only five thirty, and if he took a cab from the airport to the motel, had a shower and freshened up, there would still be plenty of time to have dinner downtown and go to the famous club.

Once in the terminal he collected his bags and walked outside into the warm heavy air of Austin. He reached into his inside jacket pocket and took out the card of the motel. A guy he'd met in Chicago had recommended it to him. 'It's a great place,' the man had said, 'and really gives you the atmosphere I think you're looking for.'

'The Lone Star Motel, please,' he said to the taxi driver.

*   *   *

It was not that she wanted to hurt her family, Grace Kent thought. It was just that, well, she had felt *invisible* for so long. It was time to reclaim her life.

Take the other day, she thought, as she looked at the huge Texan landscape outside the window. It was typical.

'Honey, I thought we'd take Mom away for Christmas,' Bob had said. He had that little boy look he sometimes put on when he had a 'plan.'

'Oh,' said Grace.

There must have been something in the way she said it that made him want to explain, because he said, 'Now that Dad's gone, it'll be lonely for her, and I think it's better to get away, you know, from the house. And maybe Lucy and

Chip would like to come over too. After all, we don't know how long she's going to be around . . .'

Grace wondered why it was that Bob's mother was somehow more important than her own parents, who were both still alive.

'I'm just mentioning it,' said Bob, realising now that they should discuss it, 'because I think we'll need to plan ahead . . .' His voice died away.

The thought of spending a vacation with Bob's mother, the quick-tempered Kate, made Grace's heart sink. And then add her own daughter Lucy, now twenty and living away from home for the first time and enjoying her new-found freedom. She would be moody and bad-tempered at having to be with family when she could be with her new friends. And *also* her son Chip, twenty-two, who would no doubt bring his latest girlfriend, and who was always moody and bad-tempered whatever the situation! The thought of going somewhere with all of them, being somewhere she couldn't get away from them . . .

It was her fault, she thought. She must have made them like this.

Grace smiled to herself through the bus window. There would have to be changes. She would go back to work, find herself something to get absorbed in, something apart from the family. Enough was enough. The kids had grown up; they could look after themselves.

The bus was approaching Austin. She would find herself a motel, settle in and phone Bob. It wasn't fair of her to let him and the kids think she was dead. She would explain things to him. That she needed a week or two just to think things through. She just needed a little time and distance to think about what she wanted to do, how she wanted things to, well, change.

Yes, it was time to reclaim her life.

*   *   *

Being defence attaché for Central America was not exactly the best job for a colonel in the British Army. Tim Parker's colleagues had smiled when they heard of the posting, as if to say, 'Well, that's got rid of him, then.'

But, thought the colonel, as he settled into his business class seat from Guatemala City to Austin via Dallas, that's where they had been wrong. The colonel was a strong believer in doing a good job, whatever the situation. He had quickly worked out there were two things that he had to work on in the region. The first was projects which were principally non-political, such as army education. The second was security. He had decided early on that he would make a name for himself in both.

He had a way of being in the right place at the right time. Security had become a priority since the terrorist attack on New York in September 2001, especially for the Americans, and the colonel's expertise was suddenly very much in demand. This had put the British Army on the map in the region and beyond, and his superiors at the Ministry of Defence were happy with him. It was a fitting end to a very good career.

The colonel reached into his briefcase and took out his papers to read through the arrangements for the conference. It was being held at a place called the Driskill Hotel. It seemed to be one of the biggest hotels in the city, and from the map it looked like it was right in the centre.

The colonel was not a believer in five-star hotels. 'They make you soft,' he always said to his wife. 'I can sleep anywhere.' Victoria didn't argue with him, though when they went on holiday she would have preferred to stay in top-class hotels, rather than the guesthouses where they usually ended up. 'Besides,' he had said to her before his trip to Austin, 'what better opportunity for a terrorist who wants to kill two hundred security experts than to have them all stay together in one hotel?' Well, she had to admit he had a point.

He had asked the organisers to find him somewhere up near Congress Avenue. 'A small hotel will do,' he had said, 'or a motel. As long as it's clean.'

He looked again at the arrangements. The Lone Star Motel was where he would stay for the next few nights. Well, it sounded very Texan, he thought and, best of all, it looked from the map to be not too far from Congress Avenue and the bridge where the bats hung before their nightly flight.

The conference didn't start until tomorrow. Tonight, he thought, he would have an early dinner, perhaps downtown. Then he would go back to Congress Avenue and go bat-spotting. It said in all the guidebooks that the best time to see them was around eight or eight thirty in the evening.

The colonel smiled to himself. There was still an hour or two before he arrived in Austin. He opened his briefcase and took out a book. He smiled as he settled down to read *A Guide to the Bats of North and South America*.

*   *   *

In San Antonio, Joe Stefano's wife Rita was worried. Joe

always met her on Monday after work. Monday was the day he finished early at the hotel. At about ten minutes to five he usually parked his Dodge truck outside the dress shop where she worked on Jefferson Street and waited for her.

Sometimes they went to see a movie at a theatre downtown. Sometimes they went to a bar for margaritas and then for dinner at a restaurant. Rita loved Italian food and San Antonio had some good places to eat. Monday was a good night to go out downtown; most people stayed at home, so the traffic wasn't too bad. Sometimes Rita and Joe just went home too. It was a fifteen-mile drive to their house outside the city.

This Monday, Rita came out of the dress shop at the usual time. She was a slim young woman with short black hair; people said she looked like the young Audrey Hepburn. In her dream life, Joe was Gregory Peck. She thought that his temper and his violence were things that the love of a good woman could make disappear.

She looked around the crowded street, but the Dodge wasn't there. Oh well, maybe he was a few minutes late; the traffic was always bad in the city these days. She waited on the sidewalk. It was still hot and she started to feel uncomfortable. She looked at her watch again. Ten past five. Where was he? She rang the hotel. No, he wasn't there. They put him onto the kitchen manager. 'No, he hasn't been here the whole day, Mrs Stefano. Matter of fact, he won't be coming back. I fired him on Friday. You mean to say he didn't tell . . .'

Rita Stefano hung up. Fired! He hadn't said anything! How dare he! Her face went red with anger. Joe had come out of prison only nine months ago, after serving two years for attacking someone. He had mixed with the wrong people, Rita thought; she just knew he wasn't a bad man in himself. Far from it. Anyway, he had come out of jail and she'd helped him get the job at the hotel. They had been lucky. It was the couple's chance to make a new start, to forget about the past. Rita had thought everything was going well, but now she started thinking about it, he had been very tense at the weekend. Kind of wound up. In fact, he'd seemed very tense for the past week or so.

'My God, where is he?' She waited and waited. Perhaps there'd been an accident. Perhaps he was at the hospital . . . 'Oh my God, perhaps he's dead,' she thought. She tried to remain calm.

At a quarter to six she couldn't wait any longer. She rang the police. 'No, ma'am,' said the police officer, 'we don't have any report of an accident to Joe Stefano.' By now she was beside herself with worry; she just couldn't understand it. She went home and waited. And waited.

*   *   *

At half past eight that Monday morning, Joe Stefano had driven his Dodge truck into a parking lot in downtown San Antonio. He wore blue trousers and a T-shirt under a thin jacket.

Joe got out of his car and walked the ten minutes to the bus station. It was hot but he walked quickly. He felt like he was going to explode. At the bus station he went into the ticket office.

Joe Stefano didn't have any particular reason to go to Austin. He just had to get away, get away from San Antonio, get away from it all. That stupid boss at the hotel who'd sacked him, his father-in-law, his stupid life. Get away from Rita, before he hurt her. Get away from his own powerlessness. Just get away.

'A ticket to Austin,' he said to the man in the ticket office.

*　　*　　*

There is no doubt that the Lone Star Motel in Austin, Texas is different. It seems to have more going for it than a regular motel. The sign outside it, pointing upwards, flashes: 'So close yet so far out.' It looks like the kind of place where Elvis Presley had parties in the 1950s. The blues singer Janis Joplin had probably stayed there. There is more than a hint of guilty pleasure about it. The rooms are pink and blue and the air conditioning is noisy but efficient. The swimming pool has cactus plants around it.

It is a place where anything might happen.

But even for a place as full of potential as the Lone Star Motel, the particular set of circumstances that threw it together with Paul Boyle, Grace Kent, Colonel Tim Parker and Joe Stefano were unfortunate to say the least.

When Joe Stefano walked into the Lone Star Motel early that summer evening, he didn't plan to use the gun he had in his jacket. He could feel it against his chest. It just made him feel better, knowing it was there. But when the clerk at reception said that the motel was full, something inside Joe broke.

When he took out his gun and went crazy, shooting everyone dead in the reception area of the motel, he didn't know who his victims were. He didn't ask whether they were aware that life is a precious thing, beautiful and pitilessly brief. He didn't ask whether they had had time to say goodbye to their loved ones, tell them, 'I love you.' He didn't know the stories that had led them to the Lone Star Motel that warm evening in late August. He didn't know that things were left well, unfinished, kind of untidy.

He didn't give them time to realise that the Lone Star Motel was their final destination, their end point.